The Elements of Ethics

The
Elements
of
Ethics

for Professionals

W. Brad Johnson and Charles R. Ridley

First published in 2008 by PALGRAVE MACMILLAN® in the
United States—a division of St. Martin's Press LLC, 175 Fifth
Avenue, New York, NY 10010.

Where this book is distributed in the UK, Europe and the rest of
the world, this is by Palgrave Macmillan, a division of Macmillan
Publishers Limited, registered in England, company number
785998, of Houndmills, Basingstoke, Hampshire RG21 6XS.

Palgrave Macmillan is the global academic imprint of the above
companies and has companies and representatives throughout the
world.

Palgrave® and Macmillan® are registered trademarks in the United
States, the United Kingdom, Europe and other countries.

ISBN-13: 978-0-230-60391-2
ISBN-10: 0-230-60391-2

Library of Congress Cataloging-in-Publication Data
Johnson, W. Brad.
    The elements of ethics : for professionals / W. Brad Johnson,
Charles R. Ridley.
        p.   cm.
    Includes bibliographical references and index.
    ISBN 0-230-60391-2
    1. Professional ethics.   I. Ridley, Charles R.   II. Title.
BJ1725.J64   2008
174—dc22

                                                    2008015920

A catalogue record of the book is available from the British Library.

Design by Letra Libre

First edition: October 2008
10   9   8   7   6   5   4   3   2   1
Printed in the United States of America.

Dedicated to

Rachel Johnson, Laura Johnson,
Annabell Ridley, and Mary Ridley,

each of whom is the embodiment of character and integrity

Contents

Acknowledgments

Once again we thank Toby Wahl, acquisitions editor at Palgrave Macmillan. Toby has been a loyal friend and ardent advocate of our *elements* books. We appreciate you.

I am grateful to several good colleagues who are living models of virtue. In their daily lives, each of these people offers a glimpse of ethics embodied. They include Art Athens, Dennis Balog, Jeff Barnett, Tim Beal, Steve Behnke, Betsy Holmes, Carol Mullen, Rick Ruble, Jim Singleton, and Steve Trainor. Thanks to each of you for providing inspiration for these elements. And special thanks go to my friend and mentor, Chuck Ridley. He models the ethical life and imbued this project with a sense of meaning.

—W. Brad Johnson
Annapolis, Maryland

I am indebted to so many people. A core circle of special friends and colleagues includes John Wasem, Pearl Barner, Rosaland Morgan, Gwendolyn Stout, Larry and Kaitlyn Picou, Marianne Mitchell, Samuel Butler, Bruce and Renee Rose, Earl Ridley, and Robert Logan. Each of you is significant in my life. And I would like to acknowledge my former student, Brad Johnson, who has become my colleague, life-long friend, and collaborator. I am proud of you as an accomplished professional but more so as a person of high character.

—Charles R. Ridley
College Station, Texas

Preface

We are discussing no small matter, but how we ought to live.
                                        Socrates, in Plato's Republic

This is a short book but not because there is little to say about ethics. Professionals of all stripes function in a society defined by creeping relativism, increasingly complex ethical quandaries, and a public that is weary of the unscrupulous—and sometimes shocking—behavior of people in positions of power. When professionals fail to abide by bedrock ethical principles and fundamental moral virtues, the quality of their performance goes down, claims of malpractice soar, cynicism and defensiveness become commonplace, and the cost of doing business goes up. Ethical challenges are notorious for stimulating powerful emotions such as anxiety, anger, and unnerving confusion. They also can lead to counterproductive behaviors such as denial, avoidance, and rationalization. And far too often, otherwise upstanding professionals worsen ethical transgressions by lying or blaming others for their own missteps. In this unsavory environment, everyone pays a price.

Being a professional with good ethics is hard work. Professional conundrums and ethical quandaries often defy easy answers. Working hard at having good ethics requires continuous care and reflection. We should appreciate the hard work for what it really is: a process, not an outcome. A firm commitment to doing what is ethically right—the very definition of integrity—demands consistent attention to one's conduct in relationships. Professionals should not consider it an act of heroism, something out of the ordinary, to hold themselves to high ethical standards. Holding oneself to high standards in the realm of ethics should be the norm. We should expect that those who have earned the right to be called professionals have accepted the ethical responsibilities that go along with their positions. Nevertheless, professionals who set high standards for themselves and live by them have a priceless achievement. It is earned. But don't be fooled. A reputation for high ethical conduct can take a lifetime to earn and can be destroyed with one swift ethical infraction.

Traveling down the ethical high road can be a lonely experience. The pressures to forsake one's ethics can be horrendous. Professionals who model ethically inappropriate conduct are plentiful, while the rewards for ethically exemplary conduct are not always apparent. In light of these challenges, the need to assist professionals could not be greater.

In this book, we zero in on the essential elements of ethics for professionals. Our purpose is to distill the voluminous research, theory, and philosophical underpinnings of ethics into a pithy, pragmatic resource. The elements are relevant to professionals in every field. We assume that our readers are sincerely invested in furthering the welfare of the people they serve—that they are committed to "doing the right thing," as it were. We hone in on the nuts and bolts of professional ethics, while we avoid tired clichés and philosophical mumbo jumbo. We offer concrete strategies for becoming deliberate and proactive in protecting the rights and interests of those we serve.

As in our first book of elements—*The Elements of Mentoring* (Johnson & Ridley, 2004)—in this book we follow the example of our writing heroes, William Strunk and E. B. White. In their classic, *The Elements of Style* (Strunk & White, 2000), Strunk and White set the standard for pithy writing. They cautioned writers to omit needless words and seek parsimony in every sentence. Then they set the bar high by putting into practice the message they preached. In trying to stay with their philosophy, a book on the crucial elements of ethics should contain no unnecessary verbiage. We hope that Strunk and White would judge this volume as clearing their high bar.

As we prepared to write this book, we reviewed several hundred articles, book chapters, and books on ethics. Many of these were philosophical volumes heavy on the original works of Socrates, Aristotle, Kant, and others, while others were theoretical tomes on moral philosophy, and still others were research studies in applied ethics. We reviewed sources from the widest range of disciplines such as business, leadership, law, medicine, education, psychology, and the allied health professions. We sought the timeless and foundational principles of professional ethics and de-emphasized profession-specific nuances of ethical behavior (we insist that ethics transcends the particulars of any discipline or professional field). In determining the essential ingredients of ethical practice, we emphasized data-supported truths and avoided "popular" fads and fruitless culs-de-sac in the ethics literature. *The Elements of Ethics* avoids myth, hype, and feel-good narrative, just like it avoids black-and-white lists of do's and don'ts. There is nothing mysterious about being ethical, and we have labored to remove any mystique professionals might harbor about this endeavor.

Our own interest in ethics is both professional and personal. Brad Johnson is a professor in the Department of Leadership, Ethics, and Law at the U. S. Naval Academy and a Faculty Associate at Johns Hopkins University. An interest in ethics has been a common thread throughout his career, during which he has been a frequent teacher of graduate-level ethics courses, an author of many articles on professional ethics, and a former chair of the American Psychological Association's Ethics Committee. Charles Ridley is a professor in the doctoral program in Counseling Psychology at Texas A & M University. A Fellow of the American Psychological Association and an organizational consultant, he also teaches ethics at the graduate level. Each of us has wrestled with ethical quandaries, adjudicated ethical problems and conflicts, and experienced the anxiety, frustration, and vexation that accompany seeking the ethical high ground in a complex world. We often are called on to advise students, colleagues, and organizations grappling with ethical concerns. Some of the concerns are large, some small. But all of them are real in the experience of the people who struggle with them. Our personal experiences and professional consultations have deepened our resolve to promote excellence in ethics among professionals.

In this terse guide to professional ethics, we have distilled the vast ethics literature into 75 key elements for achieving ethical excellence. These elements should be equally relevant to students, neophyte professionals, and seasoned leaders. The elements are clustered around 11 primary themes—taking the high ground (matters of integrity); doing no harm (matters of nonmaleficence); according dignity (matters of respect); benefiting others (matters of beneficence); exercising caution (matters of prudence); caring for others (matters of compassion); seeking fairness (matters of justice); promoting autonomy (matters of self-reliance); being faithful (matters of fidelity); delivering your best (matters of excellence); and making ethical decisions (matters of sound judgment). At the end of the book, we provide a list of key references on professional ethics. These sources may be useful for scholars or professionals who want to read the ethics literature in greater detail.

Ethics—sometimes called moral philosophy—is the branch of philosophy concerned with how we ought to live. Ethics involves establishing principles of right behavior that can be translated to life and work. The study of ethics is the study of moral values, which values are most important, and which standards of morality we should require one another to adhere to. We assume that one's commitment to moral values provides a context or frame in which ethical decision making occurs. Applied ethics—the focus of this book—involves the application of moral beliefs and ethical principles to the specific problems and demands of a profession. Many professions promulgate *ethics codes*—specific standards for ethical conduct. Professional codes offer a guide and a way forward in our efforts to be moral in the practice of our profession. Practicing in accordance with your profession's code will nearly always help protect your clients and protect you against complaints or malpractice suits. But these codes are limited. They are necessary but never sufficient. Much like laws, ethics codes often are concerned with minimum standards of practice, and, like laws, they vary across jurisdictions and professions. Ethical excellence requires more than adherence to minimum standards. It demands a deeper commitment to live according to bedrock virtues and aspire to timeless principles.

There are several reasons why codes and rules for doing the "right" thing as a professional are disappointing in real-life practice: (1) Ethical quandaries are complex and their resolution often nuanced and resistant to simple rules; (2) Ethical quandaries are fluid and demand considerable flexibility on the part of the professional; (3) Professionals often encounter competing obligations to individuals, organizations, and society at large, and there often are good reasons for different courses of action; (4) Being ethical is a continuous process, not merely a right answer; and (5) Ethical decisions are made by fallible human beings, many of whom are motivated by self-interest, defensiveness, and a remarkable capacity to justify unethical courses of action.

For all of the above reasons, we encourage readers to recognize the necessity of both ethical *principles* and moral *virtues* when considering how to be ethical. Ethical principles are established rules for action or conduct in relationships with others. For example, most of us believe in the principles of beneficence (do what is best for others) and autonomy (honor others' rights to independence and self-determination). From the principle perspective, a professional might consider each rule or principle to which he or she is obligated in deciding on a course of action. From the perspective of principle ethics, the key question is: *What shall I do?* But when ethical problems are complex, when moral principles appear to dictate different courses of action, and when the professional traverses into new practice territory, the rules of navigation offered by ethics codes may not be enough. Here is where the necessity of moral virtues is clear. When operating from the perspective of moral virtues, the question becomes: *Who shall I be?* The professional not only must follow ethical principles but must indeed "be" a virtuous agent—a professional characterized by moral excellence, goodness, and righteousness. Ethical rules must be thoughtfully tempered by the wisdom of virtue. No principle has validity apart from its impact on people, and only a genuinely virtuous agent is positioned to evaluate rules in this human light. In sum, to maximize the chances that a wise ethical decision will be rendered, the professional must *both* appreciate the rules and principles governing ethical behavior and be a person who is defined by clear moral virtues such as prudence, integrity, and compassion. Because ethicists do not always agree about which facets of morality constitute principles and which are virtues, we do not attempt to separate them in this guide. In many cases, the elements may be framed by the reader as principles, virtues of character, or both.

In *The Elements of Ethics*, we introduce each element with an applied case study of an ethical professional at work. Each case study represents an amalgam of excellent professional practice we have witnessed over the years. Although each case is fictitious, each offers a clear example of the best practice in professional ethics. After summarizing the essential details of each element of ethical practice, we conclude with a terse summary of its basic ingredients—the *key components*. When faced with a conflict or quandary, readers may quickly refer to these key components for a rapid refresher on each element.

The choices we make as professionals often have surprising consequences—both for good and bad. By learning and living *The Elements of Ethics*, we hope that you will become more intentional, more thoughtful, and more confident as a moral agent in your profession. Whether you are a new member of your profession or a seasoned ambassador, we hope this guide becomes an invaluable source of encouragement and wisdom for everything you do in your personal and professional life.

The Elements of Ethics

1

Taking the High Ground

Matters of Integrity

The story of ethics for professionals begins with integrity. A commitment to ethics must start with the decision to live and work in accordance with a set of moral principles. What's more important, one's actions must be consistent with these principles at all times and in all contexts. Integrity speaks of wholeness, coherence in one's behavior, and adherence to a set of principles. Nowhere should integrity be more apparent than in the face of adversity, for therein can be found its true test.

In this first section of *The Elements of Ethics,* we distill the virtue of integrity into 13 essential elements. Professionals of all stripes must maintain congruence and transparency in their work. They make themselves accountable, protect confidentiality, and avoid inaccuracies in describing their services. Ethical professionals know their personal vulnerabilities, private agendas, and signs of emotional distress. They take steps to prevent these issues from harming their colleagues and clients as well as from taking a toll on themselves. Finally, professionals defined by integrity are quick to acknowledge their mistakes and make amends.

As a moral virtue, integrity may sound like it should come naturally. Don't be fooled. Behaving with honesty, truthfulness, and consistency can be a hard feat to accomplish. Functioning as a principled professional and adhering to a code of ethics at all times, in all places, throughout all facets of one's personal and professional life, and over the long term requires Herculean commitment. It also requires sage guidance and social support. Remember that the price of unprincipled action ultimately will be more costly than the price of integrity. The damage exacted on colleagues, constituents, your organization, your profession, and you and your family can be immeasurable. Just look at the well-publicized ethics dramas in the news. We believe that each of the following *elements* highlights the dire importance of integrity in the life of every professional.

1
Become Congruent

During a cross-country flight en route to a job interview, Amanda had a brief conversation with an older gentleman sitting next to her. When he discovered that Amanda was seeking the athletic director job at a regional university, the passenger smiled conspiratorially and whispered, "I sure hope you'll not get too wrapped up in all those NCAA rules. A lot of us fans are more interested in winning than in the details of recruiting. Don't you think smaller schools need to flex the rules now and then to compete?" Without missing a beat, Amanda looked the gentleman in the eyes and replied, "If I am hired, I can assure you that every NCAA recruiting rule will be observed and strictly enforced. The best programs win without cheating. I will hire the best coaches and give them the resources they need, but I will not tolerate rule infractions for a second." At this, the passenger raised his eyebrows, nodded, and became quiet. The next morning, Amanda was shocked to see this same gentleman sitting behind the university president's desk. She was hired on the spot.

Mirrors don't lie. When you peer at yourself in a mirror, what you see is what you get—the real, unabridged you. Your mirror might reveal a smile, youthfulness, shining white teeth, and good posture, or reveal gray hair, wrinkles, and an oversize figure. For better or for worse, your mirror tells the truth. Now suppose you could look into a psychological mirror that reflects the inner you. On the inside, we would see your likes and dislikes, preferences, prejudices, deep feelings, values, attitudes, dreams and aspirations, and personal secrets. As the mirror peels away the veneer, how would you look on the inside?

William Shakespeare, in *Hamlet*, had something to say about truthfully reflecting on who you are as a person. "To thine own self be true, / and it must follow, as the night the day, / Thou canst not then be false to any man" (*Hamlet*, Act 1, Scene 3). Being truthful with oneself is the first step on the path to becoming an ethical professional. The truth allows you to travel far along that path. Famous psychologist Carl Rogers used the term *congruence* to describe the state of being true to oneself. Consistency is the second step on the path to becoming an ethical professional. It allows you to seek harmony between your own values, beliefs, and behaviors. The ethical life requires an integrated sense of self in relationship to others. It is a fundamental consistency between moral convictions and behavior across time and situations. In essence, ethical professionals must "be" who they "are" at all times and in all relationships.

If congruence sounds simple, it's not. Being honest with ourselves and being consistent can be painful. Because of their pain, some professionals fail to "walk the talk," as it were, putting into question their real ethics. How many professionals truly are perceived by subordinates and colleagues as genuine? How many "straddle the fence" when it's time to make a hard decision? And how many behave hypocritically or act in bad faith when they think no one is looking? Here is what you should know: Congruence is an aspect of character that develops over time. Sometimes it is months and years in the making, and usually it evolves out of a process of deliberate self-reflection and openness to constructive feedback.

Why is congruence so fundamental to the ethical life? The evidence from business, education, and counseling provides an answer. Healthy relationships and interpersonal trust hinge on honesty and consistency. The colloquial saying "Say what you mean, and mean what you say" speaks to this point. When people around us find genuine harmony between our words and actions, their concern about hidden agendas or fears of manipulation are dispelled. People see us as safe, and because of their feelings of safety, they more freely lower their defenses, stop playing games, and are less prone to try to manipulate us. These responses are hard earned. They are earned through the aforementioned process of deliberate self-reflection, but we never arrive at a point whereby we are beyond another careful look at ourselves. Furthermore, going through the process requires enough comfort with who we are that there is no motivation to put on a facade.

There is another reason for becoming congruent: Incongruence is self-defeating, and it evokes unnecessary emotional pain. Unless you are a psychopath, a person who doesn't feel normal pain for wrongdoing, you will experience guilt or shame in any rift between your beliefs or between your beliefs and behaviors. Psychologist Leon Festinger (1957) proved this point in a famous series of experiments. He discovered that when people are asked to lie—to behave in violation of their own beliefs and values—they experience a powerful sense of distress and a subsequent drive to eliminate this distress by justifying their behavior. Termed *cognitive dissonance*, nearly all human beings experience this unpleasant internal state when they attempt to hold incompatible thoughts (e.g., "Lying is morally wrong" and "I can lie to make a sale now and then") or live with incompatible thoughts and behavior (e.g., "I believe protecting confidentiality is essential" and "I just divulged personal information about a colleague"). As the distance widens between our *ideal* moral self and *real* moral self, we can expect to feel greater dissonance and increasing distress.

The solution to cognitive dissonance is simple: Be truthful with yourself—however painful that might be—and act in accordance with your internal values. If you discover personal difficulty with moral congruence, then it may be time for a deliberate process of moral reckoning. It may be time to confront your incongruence. It also may be time to become an orthodox observer of the principles you claim as your own.

Key Components

- *Be clear about who you are and what you believe.*
- *Seek consistency between your emotions, values, and behavior.*
- *Remember that congruence develops over time.*
- *Understand that congruence begets freedom in people around you.*
- *Recognize that incongruence is ultimately self-defeating.*

2
Stay Transparent

As director of human resources for a Fortune 500 Company, Steven developed a reputation for innovative, effective, and cost-efficient employee assistance programs. His programs quickly garnered national attention. When other companies began to solicit his services as a consultant, Steven initially kept a low profile. He feared the moonlighting would anger his boss, even though he was conscientious in conducting the extra work outside normal business hours and off the premises of his employer. As Steven's reputation grew and more consulting came his way, his anxiety about keeping it under wraps intensified. In coming to grips with the strain resulting from his cloak-and-dagger behavior, he decided to tell his boss about the consulting. As he related the developments, he assured his boss that the outside work did not interfere with his primary job. To Steven's surprise, his boss did not get angry. Instead, he showed appreciation for Steven's honesty and, surprisingly, delighted in the national attention Steven's consulting might bring to the company. Steven's transparency not only proved to be the right approach, it freed him from his anxiety and allowed him to relax and enjoy both of his jobs.

If you look through a clean window of a house on a bright, sunny day, you can see inside clearly. The objects you see through the window are lucid. No second-guessing about their identity is necessary. The blue couch you perceive really is a blue couch; the messy desk, a messy desk; and the grandfather clock, a grandfather clock. Are you transparent? Can people see the truth about you? Or do they have to second-guess?

If you could do anything humanly possible with the complete assurance that you would not be detected or held responsible, what would you do? Be honest. When this question was posed to university students and they were allowed to respond anonymously, the most common answer was not what you would expect. The majority of responses were antisocial—the respondents would violate the rights of others or societal laws. University students' responses were nearly identical to those of convicted felons. They indicated that they would steal money, spy, or engage in promiscuous or unlawful sexual acts, or in other activities that violate their own moral commitments.

When we believe that our personal behavior is shrouded and we are free to get by without detection, we run the risk of *deindividuation* (Zimbardo, 1969). Normally restrained and inhibited behavior is released in violation of ethical rules or laws. What underlies our personal psychology when we think others won't discover our actions? Feelings of anonymity, which are also reported by members of a mob, are at the root of deindividuation. These feelings numb our normal self-awareness, causing a temporary loss of personal identity and accountability. Losing touch with our sense of self, even for a moment, is dangerous business. The siren song of perceived anonymity has the power to make us behave without inhibition and forget about outside evaluation.

Integrity hinges on transparency—openness, frankness, and a willingness to shine the light of scrutiny on everything we do. Transparency requires unwavering honesty and full disclosure. Not surprisingly, most professional organizations now require their stakeholders to disclose the nature of their relationships when conducting research or making public statements. A physician must be transparent about a relationship with a pharmaceutical company when publishing research about the efficacy of medications. The public has a right to know about the relationship so that citizens can decide whether there is a conflict of interest and make an informed choice about their medical care. Transparency does not mean indiscriminate self-disclosure, saying everything you think or feel. After all, "discretion is the better part of valor." For instance, it is not discreet to reveal trade secrets to a competitor. Transparency does mean keeping your activities above board, honoring your commitments, and clarifying the nature of your relationships.

Transparency and guardedness are contradictory. Keep in mind that as you become clandestine or evasive, people become suspicious of you. Your credibility and the trust people have in you directly relate to your transparency. Transparent professionals engender confidence and reassurance among colleagues, clients, and customers. Opaque professionals, those who are secretive, engender mistrust and suspicion. Why cast doubt on your own integrity? If you are tempted to become a closed person, ask yourself some other important questions. What are you hiding? What is the motivation behind your secrecy? What do you fear? What do you stand to gain or lose by being closed? One day you may find yourself in a position similar to Steven's: contemplating whether to self-disclose about an important matter. Asking yourself these questions might help you see the importance of staying transparent.

Key Components

- Refuse to project an image that is intended to deceive others.
- Remember that anonymity raises the risk of unethical behavior.
- Fully disclose your relevant interests and relationships up front.
- Realize that "hidden" transgressions are usually revealed in time.

3
Make Yourself Accountable

Identified early in his teaching career as a "rising star," Miguel was flattered and encouraged when, at the ripe old age of only 29, he was appointed principal of a large inner-city middle school. During Miguel's first year on the job, parents and district administrators were delighted to see a rise in student academic performance and teacher morale. But that first spring Miguel was blindsided. A routine audit revealed that the school had failed to schedule legally mandated health inspections during each of the previous three years. This failure provoked an outcry in the community, and caustic reports of negligence circulated in the local media. Immediately, Miguel shifted into high gear. He reviewed the relevant guidelines and district policies. Then he met with the superintendent of schools, assumed responsibility for the oversight, and outlined a plan of action. He committed himself to correcting the problem and addressing public criticism. Next he met with representatives of the news media and parents, again assuming responsibility for the failure. Rather than blaming his predecessor, the district, or his vice principal (the person actually responsible for inspections), Miguel admitted that in his first year on the job, he'd been overwhelmed with the demands of turning the school around and simply had not attended to that part of the job. He insisted that the blame was his and promised to correct the oversight immediately. His actions quickly quieted criticisms.

President Harry Truman had it right. On the Oval Office desk at the White House sat a plaque with an amusing but inspiring inscription: *The buck stops here.* He took great pride in personally putting those words into practice. If we paraphrase Truman's declaration, we might say something like this: *I am the one responsible for all my actions—the successes and the failures. I ultimately am accountable to myself.*

Responsible professionals—the ones who offer a transparent accounting of their performance—silence their critics and give their supporters reason to take heart. Accountability, the opposite of excuse making or blaming, is the willingness to give a credible explanation for one's decisions, judgments, and actions. To be accountable is to accept without hesitation or evasion the consequences of our behavior, which includes the good, the bad, and the ugly.

In elegant written prose, human resources consultant Susan M. Heathfield (2008) gives a vivid explanation of accountability.

Excuses for failure, excuses about your choices in life, excuses about what you feel you have accomplished fuel dysfunctional thinking—and consequently, undesirable actions and behaviors. Making excuses instead of taking one hundred percent responsibility for your actions, your thoughts, and your goals is the hallmark of people who fail to succeed. Part of the power of taking responsibility for your actions is that you silence the negative, unhelpful voice in your head. When you spend your time thinking of success and goal accomplishment, instead of making excuses, you free up emotional space formerly inhabited by negativity.

How many politicians, corporate leaders, and professional athletes hold themselves to a high standard of personal accountability? Indeed, how many of them boldly welcome the opportunity to honestly disclose their actions and take appropriate blame for their bad decisions and mistakes? How many high-profile professionals accept that accountability means taking deserved credit *and* deserved blame?

In this era of status and fame seeking, professionals of all stripes seem to be schooled in the art of passing the buck, dancing around the truth, and answering for their actions only when they are backed into a corner. The discovery of recorded messages, revealing pictures, or written notes may be required for some to own up to their transgressions, and even then they may evade the truth until their attorney assures them there are no other good options. But here is the surprise: Being accountable, especially when accompanied by sound judgment and professional competence, is likely to win you more credibility than any other professional behavior. CEOs, supervisors, share-holders, colleagues, and clients are drawn to professionals who hold themselves accountable and admit their own mistakes.

Accountability begins with accuracy. The opportunities for many professionals to improve their income or status through misrepresentation or falsification are legion. Concealing the actual nature, duration, or cost of one's services, pinning blame for a serious error on someone else, or otherwise engaging in fraudulent behavior can be profoundly tempting. Beyond an abiding commitment to integrity, the most effective antidote to such temptation simply is openness and honesty. When we truthfully disclose our thoughts and behaviors to trusted colleagues or partners, there is a precipitous decrease in the probability of shirking responsibility.

Key Components

- *Always stand ready to give an accounting of your behavior.*

- *Be accountable in both your personal and professional life.*
- *Appreciate the fact that taking responsibility engenders trust in others.*
- *Realize that full accountability silences critics and reassures stake-holders.*

4
Invite Peer Review

Olivia was a senior manager for a company specializing in the development and manufacture of innovative toys and games for children. She also had a sterling track record of testing and screening new products. Since Olivia's coming on board, the company never issued a recall or suffered financial loss due to unforeseen defects or safety problems. When someone asked about her secrets to success, Olivia was often quick to say, "I use reliable critics." When asked to elaborate, she said, "I insist that all of the company's product testing and safety screening trials are conducted by external consultants. I use only the best in the industry and those who have no allegiance to or vested interest in our company." While using only in-house experts was the industry norm, Olivia demanded a generous budget that accommodated scrupulous review from outside scientists and technicians. Understanding the sometimes subtle pressure from management to get new concepts quickly into production, Olivia took every step of precaution to guarantee integrity in the testing process. Olivia believed that opening the process to thorough and transparent peer review was essential.

Constructive feedback, possibly the most intimidating aspect of work but probably the most valuable resource at our disposal, is our friend. When the review of our work comes from competent peers, we should be quick to embrace it, rather than retreat from it as though it were an enemy. Here is a rule of thumb: If you are doing something in your professional life that you would not want your colleagues or superiors to know about, you probably shouldn't be doing it. An essential element of transparent integrity involves inviting others to observe and evaluate our professional work. Seeking peer review communicates openness, helps ensure honesty, and facilitates the meeting of high standards.

Peer review is no stranger to professors in colleges and universities. When professors present grant proposals for research funding or articles for publication, their submissions must undergo anonymous peer review by experts in their field. Scholarship that does not undergo rigorous peer review typically is not granted the same degree of credibility as peer-reviewed research. Some scholars mistakenly underestimate the importance of peer-reviewed research, but they should welcome the scrutiny. Thoughtful reviews can pinpoint strengths and weaknesses as well as errors and oversights. They also can provide guidance in how to improve one's work.

As humans, we are unwise to expect flawless performance or the capacity to keep temptation forever at bay. We do have flaws, and we will be tempted. Therefore, we should welcome peer review. Fighting the urge to respond to peer review with defensiveness and distrust, we should consider it a profound opportunity. If the review is appropriate, confidentiality will be ensured, and proprietary information will be protected. Most professionals have an ethical obligation to participate in peer evaluation of their work.

What happens to professionals who eschew open review by colleagues? Evidence from the front page of the daily newspaper makes it all too clear. No one stands above the potential for deception, evasion, and out-and-out lying. When money, power, success, or prestige are on the line, even highly regarded professionals have been found to cut corners, falsify data, plagiarize, or dupe the public, clients, and their own families. In failing to submit ourselves to rigorous scrutiny, we may find the temptation to take unfair or illegal advantage too beguiling to resist.

Here is an interesting observation: In accepting peer review as an ethical obligation and making it a habit, we not only reduce the risk of behaving inappropriately, we improve the quality of our work. By submitting ourselves to review, we arrange unvarnished criticism and invaluable neutral observation. The quality, appropriateness, and even the spirit of our work are put to the test. Peer review may keep you on the ethical straight and narrow while simultaneously encouraging personal reflection, collaboration, and professional development. One caveat about effective peer review is in the selection of reviewers.

Avoid cronies and "yes people." Seek competent and trustworthy colleagues who have a reputation for propriety and wisdom. Ask for uncompromising forthrightness in the evaluation of your work.

Finally, don't forget that excellent peer-review relationships are a two-way street. When the need arises, be sure to reciprocate the favor with honest evaluations of your colleagues' work. When colleagues ask for your opinion—whether it is about their conduct, decisions, or work products—take their request seriously, respect confidentiality, never disseminate their ideas or findings without their consent, and, by all means, tell the truth and pull no punches. Just as you expect your colleagues to pull you back from the ethical edges with timely warnings and clear criticism, be sure to offer equally constructive criticism when it is your turn. Remember that only honest feedback is helpful.

Key Components

- *Deepen professional accountability by arranging peer review of your work.*
- *Retain colleagues and experts with a reputation for wisdom and confidentiality.*
- *Identify defensiveness and evasion as warning signs that peer review is needed.*
- *Take collegial feedback seriously, and use it to avoid ethical transgressions while improving the quality of your work.*
- *Reciprocate peer reviews with honest and confidential feedback to colleagues.*

5

Present Your Credentials and Services Accurately

As a psychotherapist and popular speaker, Shaun frequently found himself having to clarify the exact nature of his credentials and temper others' unrealistic claims about his services. On the eve of a major workshop to be conducted for more than 1,000 mental health professionals, Shaun discovered that the promotional materials made reference to his "doctorate in psychology" and the "nearly miraculous" efficacy of his therapy approach for nearly any psychological problem. When the event organizer refused Shaun's request to reprint the promotional materials, Shaun began his presentation by making a public disclaimer. He told the audience that he held a master's degree, not a doctorate, and that the research evidence supported his therapeutic approach for certain disorders under certain conditions—not for all clinical problems. Several participants in the workshop already knew the real facts about Shaun's education and research. On the workshop evaluations, these individuals indicated that Shaun's unwavering integrity and clear commitment to truth in advertising had inspired them just as much as the content he presented.

Recall this embarrassing fiasco: In 2001, Notre Dame named George O'Leary as the university's new head coach of its storied football program. For O'Leary, who had been eminently successful as a coach and admired by fans, the appointment was the crowning opportunity of his career. His dream, though, quickly became a nightmare. Five days after his hire and before running a single practice, Coach O'Leary was forced to resign in disgrace. He did not hold a master's degree or play on his college football team as indicated on his résumé and exposed by the media. The glaring lies now were public. In his resignation statement, O'Leary admitted lying on his résumé as a young coach in the hopes of obtaining a job. As the years went by, expunging these fibs from his record became increasingly difficult. A statement by Notre Dame poignantly captured the sentiment such duplicity can arouse: "These inaccuracies constitute a *breach of trust* that makes it impossible to move forward in the relationship." Few things undermine relationships—personal or professional—more quickly than the revelation that a partner has lied.

Integrity demands clarity in the presentation of one's credentials, achievements, and experience. Ethical professionals refuse to inflate or misrepresent the nature or efficacy of their services. Whether motivated by egotism, inadequacy, or greed, inaccurate presentation of credentials or services always constitutes a fundamental ethical breach.

Professionals must stridently refuse the temptation of making false, deceptive, or fraudulent statements about any aspects of their work. Statements about (1) training and experience, (2) academic degrees, (3) credentials, licenses, or competence, (4) affiliations with institutions or organizations, (5) achievements, and (6) the nature and scientific basis for our services never are negotiable. Only by insisting on a full and accurate accounting of one's background and achievement can the slippery slope of misrepresentation be avoided. And remember one last thing: Creating false impressions or misunderstandings through omission or vague reporting is just as inappropriate as overt lying. These behaviors are a misrepresentation of the truth. Lying will come back to bite you, sometimes when you least expect it.

Why do professionals who seem to have it all together make false statements? There are many reasons, but three stand out. First, eager for success or financial reward, new professionals may be tempted to overstate the nature of their credentials. The long-term implications of such duplicity may not be something they consider. So be careful in how you try to "jump-start" your career. Second, some professionals struggle with integrity. Lying about their credentials, their background, and their capabilities is merely one more venue for self-serving manipulation. Third, some professionals try to bolster their deflated egos. Their narcissistic need for tribute, admiration, and adulation makes lying about their experiences and accomplishments nearly intoxicating. Consider the strange phenomenon of fake Navy SEALs. Several organizations now track down and expose thousands of men each year who lie on their résumés, claiming prior service with the Special Forces. The motivation for the fakery is often a desperate effort to compensate for a personal sense of inadequacy.

But the potential for aggrandizement, power, and fame resides in all of us. During your career, you will encounter endless opportunities to find short-term success through inflation, exaggeration, and deception. Whether claiming degrees from phony diploma mills, overstating your achievements, or allowing inaccuracies to go uncorrected, many among us will succumb to this temptation.

Therefore, vigilance to the dangers of misrepresentation can never be too great.

Key Components

- *Avoid making any false or deceptive statement about yourself or your services.*
- *Take responsibility to ensure that any work done or statement made on your behalf is fully accurate.*
- *Acknowledge and guard against the human tendency to self-aggrandize.*
- *Recognize that deception or duplicity in any form sabotages professional relationships.*

6
Ensure Your Personal Fitness to Practice (Maintain Self-Care)

Yvonne was a rising star in her law firm. A highly recruited graduate of an Ivy League law school, she quickly established herself as a front-runner for early promotion to partner. Yvonne was held in high esteem by colleagues, feared by opponents in the courtroom, and respected in the legal community for her professionalism and attention to detail. With all her early successes, Yvonne was not well prepared, however, for the sudden death of her parents in an automobile accident. The resulting need to assume responsibility for two younger siblings and battle her depression in the months that followed proved to be too much. Her initial effort to maintain a regular work schedule was valiant. It was vintage Yvonne at work. But to her consternation, it wasn't long before she recognized that she was emotionally disengaged, overwhelmed, and, for the first time in her life, falling below her own standards of performance. It just was not like her to be ill prepared for meetings and proceedings. After consulting with two trusted colleagues and a close friend, she decided to take a leave of absence, followed by a return in half-time status. She accepted that this decision probably meant the end of her ambition for partner status. Although this was not an easy pill to swallow, she came to the conclusion that her ethical obligations to clients, her

own health, and her ability to be an effective caretaker demanded this
course of action. Not only was she tremendously relieved by this decision, she
received strong support from the firm's partners.

Integrity dictates that you admit when you are vulnerable to distress, fatigue, burnout, and impairment. Over the course of your professional life, it would be highly unusual to avoid occasional episodes
of personal loss, relationship disturbance, or emotional turmoil. The
question is not: Will distressing episodes occur? The more realistic
questions are: When distressing episodes occur, will you be aware of
them? Will you take appropriate action? Will you take the necessary
steps to ensure that those with whom you engage professionally will
not be harmed by your distress?

Acting with integrity requires self-awareness and blatant honesty
when it comes to competence and personal psychological fitness. Ensuring adequate emotional health is a deeply personal matter. With
few professions routinely screening its members for impairments,
professionals must make an abiding personal commitment to their
own mental health. Busy professionals are tempted to ignore, minimize, or rationalize signs of impairment. Going through a divorce,
receiving a poor performance appraisal on the job, managing a
chronic physical illness, or balancing the stressful demands of raising
children, paying bills, and caring for aging parents can put professionals at risk for poor performance on the job, diminished energy,
and perhaps incapacitation. When professionals are out of touch
with their emotional lives, equate help-seeking or self-care with
weakness, or remain determined to keep turmoil and distress private,
they are making themselves substantially more vulnerable to ethically
inappropriate behavior.

When circumstances, stressors, or phases of life conspire to create
the risk of impairment, each of us has an ethical obligation to take
action. We must be proactive about prevention and responsive in remediation. A number of proven steps help ensure fitness: (1) Begin
by admitting that you are human and like other humans, vulnerable
to distress and impairment; (2) Practice excellence in self-care, in-

cluding exercise, leisure time, spiritual reflection, and social relationships; (3) Develop strong collegial relationships so that trusted colleagues will confront you, support you, or cover for you if time off is necessary; (4) Know your limits, and say no when you become overextended; (5) Be alert to warning signs of distress such as emotional outbursts, fatigue, sleep disturbance, conflicts in relationships, missed appointments, lowered concentration, and forgetfulness; (6) Seek consultation from trusted friends and colleagues when you are distressed, and take their constructive feedback to heart; (7) Seek professional help when needed—especially if emotional distress or substance use become pronounced.

Ask yourself these important questions. If your impairment results in unprofessional conduct, would a jury of your peers conclude that you should have known that your personal problems might interfere with your professionalism? Because of the clear signs of impairment, would they agree that you took appropriate measures? Would they question why you did not obtain professional consultation or limit or suspend your professional activities until your impairment was resolved? In essence, was your response to your own distress adequate?

Being a professional requires adequate self-care. Self-awareness, self-regulation, intentional life balance, and an appreciation of one's vulnerabilities are essential. Remain vigilant to evidence of dysfunction in your professional life, and be proactive in addressing it.

Key Components

- *Appreciate your human vulnerability to distress and impairment.*
- *Maintain balance between work and leisure.*
- *Be vigilant and responsive to signs of impairment; don't ignore or minimize red flags.*
- *Maintain close connections to colleagues who will confront and assist you.*
- *Seek professional consultation if personal distress threatens to diminish your professionalism or create risk for those you serve.*

7
Protect Confidential Information

*At the age of 40, Henry left an international accounting firm and estab-
lished a lucrative financial planning service. Located near Hollywood,
California, Henry's service attracted many clients who were associated
with the entertainment industry, and many of them referred their friends.
Henry recognized early on that strict protection of each client's privacy and
confidentiality would be essential to the health of his business. Aware that
many of his clients were acquainted, Henry was zealous about refraining
from any discussion of his clientele. He insisted that his office staff abide by
equally assiduous discretion. When a client attempted to elicit information
about a friend or casually probe Henry about his familiarity with a certain
star, he would smile and politely say, "I have many interesting clients, and
I endeavor to guard each client's privacy with the same vigor that I safeguard yours." Although they sometimes were annoyed by his ironclad commitment to confidentiality, Henry's clients actually were most impressed
with his propriety. It is of interest that the more tight lipped he was, the
more business he generated.*

During World War II, the Department of Defense recognized the
security risks associated with casual or inadvertent disclosures about
military operations. In response, a series of posters was printed and
displayed in areas frequented by military personnel. The posters—
depicting a burning ship slipping beneath the waves—carried the
now iconic slogan Loose Lips Sink Ships! Of course, this slogan has
broader implications. Loose lips also sink companies, relationships,
and professional reputations.

Professionals have a fundamental obligation to protect confidential information disclosed to them in the course of their work.
Clients and others with whom professionals work assume that the
information they share will be protected and never revealed unless
they make a special request. Maintaining confidentiality is central to
professionalism and inextricably linked to respect and trust. This
makes profound sense when one considers that information shared in
confidence frequently poses a threat to or reveals some vulnerability
in the person disclosing it. Confidential information is inherently

private, intimate, and secret. The decision to disclose delicate matters to a professional is seldom made lightly and always communicates some level of trust. The trust relates to professionals exercising the utmost discretion in guarding the information. Confidentiality is considered so pivotal—even sacrosanct—in some professions that many jurisdictions afford legal privilege to information shared with a professional (e.g., lawyer, clergy, medical provider).

But if confidentiality is so essential to professionalism, why is broken confidence so pervasive? Why are secrets so hard to keep? Human history is replete with violations of confidence. Ethics committees in numerous professions have their hands full adjudicating violations of confidentiality. Here are just a few of the many reasons confidentiality is violated:

- *Social Gratification:* Many of us are enticed by the attention and celebrity associated with revealing "juicy" tidbits about a well-known person.

- *Inattentiveness:* Some of us simply fail to pay careful attention to propriety and lack discretion in our conversations or public statements.

- *Failure to Address Conflicting Demands:* Legal statutes, regulations, or local policy may conflict directly with our obligation to protect confidentiality. Failure to make every effort to resolve this conflict in the best interests of a client constitutes an ethical infraction.

- *Poor Planning:* Professionals must ensure that confidential records are carefully safeguarded, regardless of the medium in which they are stored. Further, professionals are obligated to ensure that their office staff is equally discreet and well trained in the area of preserving confidence.

- *Failure to Discuss Limits:* In many professions and jurisdictions, there are limits to confidentiality or times when a professional is obligated by law to disclose confidential information in spite of the client's wishes to the contrary. For instance, a legal subpoena or direct threat of harm to others may trigger mandatory disclosure in some states. Here is the imperative: Clients

must be informed of any limits to confidentiality at the outset
of the relationship.

Protecting confidential information requires prudence. Professionals
who are thoughtful and reflective think before they speak. Colleagues,
friends, and family members know them as reticent to discuss details
about their work. At social events, ethical professionals are mindful of
the power of substances to lower their defenses. They are reluctant to
discuss work-related matters in these circumstances. Finally, professionals must be conscientious in avoiding inadvertent disclosure of confidential information in the course of public presentations, teaching, or
media interviews. In these situations, professionals have two choices.
They either secure written permission from clients to make reference to
them in public statements, or they change enough of the details related
to a specific case, making it impossible for even the client's family members to identify the person in the professional's illustrations.

Professionals have *fiduciary* relationships with their clients. This
means that they function as trustees for clients. Fiduciary relationships always presume a relationship characterized by trust, confidence, and responsibility. Protecting clients' confidence stands at the
very heart of the fiduciary relationship.

Key Components

- *Be ever vigilant to protecting client confidentiality.*
- *Remember that propriety and discretion are key elements of trust.*
- *Carefully train your staff and create systems to protect client confi-
  dentiality.*
- *Resist the temptation to discuss work in any extrawork context.*

8
Know Your Moral Vulnerabilities

*As a psychiatrist in private practice, Anthony worked hard at adhering to
the highest ethical standards in his profession. His urban clientele included*

a substantial number of attractive, interesting, and intelligent women whom he often saw weekly. Many of them were in long-term psychotherapy. After what Anthony described as several "near misses," meaning that he had entertained romantic fantasies about some of his patients and had come close to blurring professional boundaries with a couple of them, he sought consultation with a highly respected and seasoned psychiatrist in the city. After several of his own "sessions," Anthony began to see that while his feelings of attraction were normal in many regards, his willingness to even consider violating the strict ethical prohibition against sexual relationships with patients was indicative of several personal vulnerabilities: loneliness, a dissatisfying marriage, and a powerful need to be validated by women. Thankful he had been spared a serious ethical transgression, Anthony became considerably more vigilant regarding his approach to female clients, and he continued to receive periodic consultation.

No one can claim not to have weaknesses. From the mightiest of men and women to the meekest, having vulnerabilities comes with the territory of being human. Yet having a weakness is not the most serious problem for most people. Ignoring weakness, discounting vulnerability, and behaving like one is invincible is a more serious problem. It can be fatal.

Greek mythology reminds us that, in spite of overall strength, a single vulnerability—when overlooked—can lead to a downfall. Achilles was reputedly the bravest hero in the Trojan War. His mother, Thetis, attempted to ensure his immortality by dipping him in the river Styx when he was an infant. As an adult, Achilles remained unaware that the heel his mother had grasped while dipping him in the river remained a source of vulnerability. In the heat of battle, Achilles died from a wound to his heel, allegedly from a poisonous arrow shot by Paris. The real tragedy is not simply that he died. His death actually was preventable. Achilles remained unaware of his vulnerability until the moment just before his death.

The myth of Achilles is a metaphor of human frailty. In addition to physical vulnerability, ignored personal shortcomings of any nature can lead to downfall. With good reason, Socrates said: *Know thyself.* Knowledge is power, and self-knowledge gives us a powerful competitive edge. Authentic self-knowledge causes us to respect our liabilities as well as assets, weaknesses as well as strengths. Professionals who fail to acknowledge their moral vulnerabilities, their propensity to ethical misconduct, are ticking time bombs—professional tragedies waiting to happen. On this theme, the novelist D. H. Lawrence wrote, "This is the very worst wickedness, that we refuse to acknowledge the passionate evil that is in all of us. That makes us secret and rotten" (1915).

Unfortunately, human beings are notorious for overestimating their own goodness and underestimating their failings. Such self-delusion takes shape in the form of denial or minimization of our shadier sides. The *self-serving bias,* a firmly established principle in social psychology, substantiates the point. Ask ordinary business-people about their morals and ethics. On a scale ranging from 1 to 100 (100 being perfect), 50 percent rated themselves at 90 or above. Only 11 percent rated themselves at 74 or lower (Lovett, 1997). Moreover, in the general population, the majority rates itself as well above average on professional competence, moral virtue, intelligence, tolerance, and even driving. Ironically, the majority cannot be above average. Just check out the ethics of people at work, or jump into your car and take a short drive. Our self-serving bias leads to a dangerous *illusory optimism.* In overlooking our vulnerability, we fail to take appropriate measures to protect ourselves from our own moral weak spots.

Superman is a better model than Achilles of how to handle imperfection. His heroism rested on a keen self-awareness, accepting that he was vulnerable to Kryptonite. This understanding of his weakness was actually an asset. Keeping this understanding in the forefront of conscious awareness, he always took the necessary precautions to avoid contact with the substance. In which area of moral thought and ethical behavior do you struggle the most? Is it dishonesty, unfairness, greed, or impulsivity? Think about your mistakes and transgressions. Is there a pattern? What are the common threads in your indiscretions? What circumstances and temptations trip you up? What is your Achilles heel, and what is your Kryptonite?

Developing self-awareness, followed by corrective action, is the most reliable antidote to overcoming your vulnerabilities. As Harry

Truman said, "Humility is to make a right estimate of oneself." So how can we combat the self-serving bias and soberly appreciate both our strengths and weaknesses? Give your vulnerabilities a name. Look at the patterns and common threads that cause you problems. And then accept responsibility, taking deliberate corrective action. Finally, ask someone you trust to help keep you honest. Nothing makes it harder to slip into indiscretion than the echo of a friend's voice in your head or a face-to-face confrontation with a colleague.

Key Components

- *Recognize your own moral vulnerabilities.*
- *Beware of the insidious effects of the self-serving bias; refuse to deny imperfections.*
- *Seek self-awareness and take time to reflect on your professional behavior.*
- *Ask trusted colleagues to help keep you honest.*

9
Identify Your Private Agendas

A midcareer nursing supervisor, Tamara was well respected by peers, trusted by subordinates, and rumored to be a prime candidate for the nursing director position in the hospital. When a few members of the staff began to float rumors and innuendos about the excessive drinking of another nursing supervisor, Tamara began her own investigation. She collected eye-witness accounts and evidence of missed work shifts ostensibly resulting from excessive drinking. After gathering enough evidence to make the case for an alcohol problem, Tamara marched into the nursing director's office and issued a complaint. The complaint triggered a formal evaluation and temporary suspension of the supervisor's contact with patients. Only after seeing the serious fallout from her actions and her colleague's life put into further disarray did Tamara come to a rude awakening. She had never spoken to her colleague about her concerns nor offered any collegial support. The ethics code of the profession encourages informal resolution of colleague impairment whenever possible. Tamara was ashamed to recognize the hidden agenda now staring her in the face. She sought elimination of a prime rival for the nursing director position under the auspices of her concern for patient well being. As someone who stood to gain from her colleague's downfall, Tamara had manifested her lack of integrity in her behavior. After this crisis of self-realization, she admitted her inappropriate actions to her peer and superior, following up with an apology.

Try running a business meeting without an agenda, and you go nowhere. More than likely, the meeting will degenerate into a free-for-all. Then try running a business meeting with a public agenda, but whose items are not the ones your colleagues believe should be given priority. More than likely, the meeting will erupt into conflict. Finally, try running a meeting in which your real agenda is private, your colleagues really do not know what is at stake. If your colleagues eventually catch on, more than likely, they will feel your tactics are cunning and deceptive.

All of us have agendas—aspirations, goals, and plans. Some of our agendas are public; others, private. In professional relationships, public agendas can foster collaboration; private or hidden agendas can foster ill will, especially if they are undergirded by ulterior motives. Most of us can recount an experience when we were the subject of someone's duplicitous intent. The intent was to dupe us, get over on us, or manipulate us for the other person's benefit. Agendas wield powerful social influence, and unscrupulous agendas undermine professional relationships.

All of us entertain hundreds of private thoughts and wishes. Our everyday fantasies generally are innocuous and seldom pose a threat to our colleagues. Private agendas are different. Rooted in deception, they are schemes—sometimes planned in great detail—to give one an unfair advantage. A jury of our peers probably would label them as unfair, unethical, and even treacherous. By concealing their aims, people who have private agendas attempt to fly under everyone else's radar screen.

Tamara's agenda was to advance her career. She used deception to undermine a colleague. Using the ruse of accountability and concern for patient well-being, Tamara ignored forthrightness as an ethical obligation. She jumped ahead of herself, bypassing any attempt at informal resolution with her impaired colleague. Certainly, substance abuse is serious, and, certainly, concern for patient well-being is preeminent. However, whenever possible, direct engagement with and supportive interventions for impaired colleagues are preferable to accusations or formal complaints. This preference is especially obligatory when no harm has occurred. And here is a paradox: In the case of Tamara, her misguided effort at resolving an ethical situation was itself ethically inappropriate.

Sometimes professionals are so self-absorbed, so self-serving, or so ambitious that they get stuck in rationalization. They are in denial because their real motives flow below the level of conscious awareness. Sigmund Freud was on point here; he believed that many of our impulses and wishes are banished from consciousness principally because they reveal unsavory aspects of our own character. The onus then is on us to watch for *secondary gains*—the unspoken benefits stemming from our deceptive maneuvers. An unexplained physical problem allowing us to miss work or generate sympathy, the reporting of a colleague for an infraction of policy that increases our status or chances for promotion, "forgetting" to give full disclosure to clients resulting in the collection of higher fees—these are some of the secondary gains lurking behind the veneer of our so-called professional behavior.

The inescapable conclusion is that all of us must be responsible for identifying our agendas, looking them in the eye, remaining receptive when colleagues point them out, and ensuring that they do not adversely impact the people we encounter. The fact that our motives might be buried does not diminish our responsibility for the outcomes of our private agendas.

Key Components

- *Accept that you probably harbor hidden agendas at times.*
- *Work at not allowing your own agendas to adversely impact those you work with.*

- *Foster collegial relationships with persons willing to point out your agendas.*
- *When in doubt, search for evidence of secondary gains in your actions.*

10
Do Not Count the Cost of Integrity

When Sang-Min began her career as a pathologist for a major medical center, her colleagues took quick note of her competence. Sang-Min's reputation for thoroughness, augmented by uncanny intuition, spread like wildfire throughout the medical and legal communities in her county. Her work was directly linked to cracking several mysterious medical and criminal cases. As her reputation grew, Sang-Min became the interest of many attorneys who attempted to retain her as an expert witness. Initially shaken by the immense pressure these lawyers exerted in their efforts to sway her testimony, Sang-Min remained resolute in presenting her findings and opinions in consistency with the evidence. She made it clear up front to all attorneys that her opinions were not for sale, and she refused work for attorneys who failed to respect her commitment to objectivity. To negate the influence of financial considerations, she required payment for her services before she conducted her examinations or provided testimony. A few less scrupulous lawyers ridiculed her, intimated that she was naïve about the real world, and caused her some emotional grief. But Sang-Min clung to her resolve, and in the end, her reputation won out. In fact, her competence was outshone only by her impeccable integrity. Demand for her services grew steadily while judges in whose courts she testified showed her the greatest respect.

In recounting the many years he was the senior American officer imprisoned in Vietnam's infamous Hanoi Hilton prisoner of war camp, Vice Admiral James Stockdale often told this story: One American officer, to get himself out of the harsh treatment, cooperated with his Vietnamese captors. While his fellow Americans held to the rules of conduct established by Admiral Stockdale, refused to cooperate with the enemy, and endured inhumane treatment, this particular officer handed over classified information, made propaganda videos for the enemy, and was rewarded with much-better living conditions. Although the officer eventually suffered a crisis of conscience, ceased his cooperation, and returned to his countrymen, he never again was fully accepted by his peers. With a reputation permanently tarnished, a few years after his repatriation to the United States he took his own life.

In contrast, consider the indomitable courage of conviction of the late Rev. Dr. Martin Luther King Jr. The slain civil rights leader, always speaking with great eloquence, once spoke these words: "I submit to you that if a man hasn't discovered something he will die for, he isn't fit to live." Standing on his conviction, Dr. King sadly paid the ultimate price at the hands of an assassin. While his assassination is stain on the pages of this country's history, Dr. King's legacy of fighting for freedom, equality, and justice lives on forever.

Integrity matters. Originating in the Latin word *integer*, which means something that acts as whole, *integrity* signifies consistency between one's moral convictions, actions, and emotions. Integrity is a characteristic of the whole of life. The hallmark of genuine integrity is a persistent commitment to do what is right, even in the face of tremendous adversity. Persisting in adherence to moral principles precisely when the going gets tough is the defining feature of integrity.

The price to be paid for integrity comes in various forms— inconvenience, self-denial, social isolation, passive-aggressive attacks, harassment, or vicious persecution. This is what can happen to you when you tell the truth, refuse to cheat, condemn fraudulent activity, criticize mismanagement, or otherwise take the ethical high road. Certainly, we are not suggesting that you should have to pay with your life, as in the case of Dr. King. The ostracized "whistle-blower" illustrates what is more likely to happen. In the short term, integrity may feel like a bad investment. Honesty, transparency, and assiduous regard for the best interests of others may mean lower profits, less personal pleasure, and more hours at work. While integrity is costly, a failure in integrity is infinitely more costly, as in the case of the officer who could not live with himself.

Although hard-earned, a career defined by integrity is likely to produce a massive return on your investment in the long run. Evidence from ethics committees and courtrooms proves this point. When professionals who have a strong track record of integrity become the subject of an ethics complaint or a criminal charge, they often get the benefit of any doubt from ethics committees or juries. They are more likely to have their charges dismissed or get lighter sentences than professionals who have a checkered history. The decision-makers place considerable weight on the person's track record, assuming that past behavior is the best predictor of future behavior.

What about the costs of integrity breakdowns? When an accountant swindles clients, executives dupe investors, clergy have extramarital affairs, or researchers fake data, consider the dire implications for the companies or organizations that employ them. Consider also the implications for the broader community of professionals whose reputations are diminished by sheer association. Real monetary value cannot be assigned to the tremendous loss of trust that typically accompanies the exposure of failures in integrity.

Do the right thing, but don't count the cost.

Key Components

- *Seek congruence between your moral convictions, actions, and emotions.*
- *Accept the fact that maintaining integrity is often difficult.*
- *Remember that integrity requires moral action in adverse circumstances.*
- *Keep in mind that integrity pays substantial long-term dividends.*
- *Don't forget that failures in integrity can be catastrophic.*

11
Rectify Missteps Immediately

As a brand-new department chair for biology at a large university, Oscar was overwhelmed with the myriad demands of the job. Having been thrust into the position on short notice, he had to retain significant teaching, advising, and research responsibilities during that hectic first semester as chair. Oscar was mortified at a department chairs meeting midway through the fall. All the other department chairs presented carefully prepared cases supporting junior members of their faculties to receive summer salary for the forthcoming year. Completely unprepared for the task, Oscar stumbled through some impromptu remarks. His lack of preparation was apparent. The junior faculty members in biology subsequently were ranked lowest on the list forwarded to the dean. After returning to his office, Oscar noticed that he somehow had overlooked a crucial e-mail spelling out the format and purpose of the meeting. He felt just awful. Immediately, he informed his junior faculty of his oversight, apologized, and promised to do everything he could to correct the problem. His next move was to schedule a meeting with the dean of the university. Again he admitted his oversight, explained the stressors involved in his transition, and then took full responsibility. The dean was sympathetic, and in the end, the biology professors were ranked competitively for summer funding. But more important, Oscar's faculty had renewed respect for him as a leader, as it would have been easy for him to cover up his mistake.

To err is human, and to admit your errors and make amends is professional. This element of integrity—admitting missteps and making amends—is another challenging task. In business, health care, and even education, our professional cultures perpetuate a defensive and self-preserving attitude. Through examples around us, we are taught to avoid admission of error. "It's not worth admitting a mistake," we are told, "if we can get by with it." Even ethics teachers sometimes encourage us to keep quiet, consult with an attorney, and circle the wagons when an error is brought into light. What happened, we wonder, to the kind of civility among professionals that dictated ownership of responsibility and acceptance of wrongdoing?

So why is it so tough to show integrity when we err? There are several reasons. First, many of us are taught to equate mistakes with failure. When we blunder, we feel intense shame and guilt. Our professional identity or sense of adequacy is so threatened that we simply will not acknowledge imperfection. It matters little whether this *zero-defect mentality* was instilled by parents, fueled by our profession, or self-inflicted. The net effect is the same—an insidious undermining of our ethics. Famous psychologist Albert Ellis reminds us that all of us are fallible, even "screwed up." Yet many of us delude ourselves with the erroneous idea that we *should* be perfect and *should* never make mistakes. Psychoanalyst Karen Horney termed this type of thinking "the tyranny of the shoulds." This mentality can thwart our best efforts at accountability. Second, some professionals are so fearful of the consequences of admitting mistakes that they avoid confession at all costs. These fear-dominated souls might concoct elaborate lies and cover-ups to escape responsibility. Their flimsy untruths amount to nothing more than a house of cards. While the house of untruth eventually tumbles down, the personal and professional collapse is more destructive. Finally, some professionals do not have good role models. It is hard to learn the art of the apology without witnessing it in others.

What is the remedy for our zero-defect thinking and our reluctance to rectify mistakes? There are several ways to increase the probability of an ethical response when—not *if*—you blow it. First, admit that you are human and consequently error prone and imperfect. Refuse to harbor delusions of grandeur that your entire professional life should be characterized by flawless perfection and, conversely, that any mistake makes you a total failure. Second, just tell the truth. This sounds so simple. For many professionals, however, it is elusive, owing to threats to their psyche about fallibility or incompetence. Be transparent about the facts and refuse to engage in obfuscation or deflection. Third, admit your mistake. Don't mince words. Practice speaking in clear, concise, and direct language regarding your mistake. Then take full responsibility. This would be a good time to sincerely thank anyone who pointed out your blunder. Fourth, apologize. There is profound power in a genuine apology. Not only is a heartfelt apology cleansing and liberating for the person who offers it, the act often diminishes acrimony and takes the edge off anger harbored by those impacted by the error. It is true that an apology cannot erase a serious mistake. An apology can create a new beginning in a professional relationship. Out of an admission of wrongdoing and a sincere apology, both parties are free to move forward with increased trust and transparency. Obviously, reconciliation requires humility.

Make no mistake, rectifying missteps requires moral courage. It can be painful to admit shortcomings, especially when we have harmed someone or when our professional identity is threatened. As an example, a group of senior physicians in England recently published a handbook of medical error in which they disclosed some of their most serious mistakes—some leading to patient death. This was a painful exercise for some of them, but they insisted that admitting mistakes and finding remedies allowed them to understand what went wrong and what changes might be required to ensure appropriate prevention.

Be an intentional model for junior professionals in this arena. When you fail, point out your failings to your subordinates, reframe the blunder as both evidence of your humanity and an opportunity to grow as a professional. When appropriate, show some humor. Accept your subordinate's failings with the same grace you extend to yourself.

Key Components

- *Admit mistakes and missteps.*
- *Refuse to tell lies, cover up, or deflect responsibility for errors.*
- *Accept your fallibility.*
- *Remember that admitting mistakes is a sign of courage, not weakness.*
- *Apologize to those you harm, and make a good-faith effort to ameliorate the damage.*

12
Stand Your Ground under Pressure

Arthur considered himself an ethical professional and an ardent adherent of his profession's code of ethics. A competent health-care administrator for

a regional hospital, Arthur was on the fast management track and des-
tined for early promotion. Trouble began when the hospital's head of ad-
ministration suddenly quit, just weeks before a key accreditation site visit.
Only days before the visitation team was to arrive on-site, everyone was
in a frenzy, trying to make sure the hospital's records were in order and
ready for review. It was at this time that Arthur discovered the former ad-
ministrator's failure to ensure that properly executed informed consent
forms were included in each patient's chart. With time ticking away and
the chief executive officer breathing down his neck and also holding the
carrot of promotion in front of him, Arthur put his ethics on hold. He
retroactively added consent forms to each chart, and in so doing, breached
ethical and legal standards. When the visitation team, astute in matters of
accreditation, made the discovery, the hospital was placed on probation,
and Arthur was fired. He was dumbfounded by how rapidly he had com-
promised himself. He had always considered himself to be impervious to
ethical transgressions.

By any standard, Michael Jordan was a phenom, arguably the
greatest basketball player of all times. Known for his incredible, almost supernatural moves on the court, he mystified spectators for
years with his seeming invincibility. When a game was on the line
and when his team needed him most, His Airness soared, taking his
game to even loftier heights.

Inevitably, there will come a time in your professional life when
you will come under pressure—not pressure to win a basketball
game but pressure to turn away from integrity. The pressure to
cave in ethically comes from numerous sources. The pressure may
come from your peers and colleagues, from a boss, from a down-
turn in your business, from your desire to make a quick buck, from
the fact that taking the shortcut or easy way out is the norm in
your organization.

In the Bible, Peter is a prime example of ethical frailty and poor
moral fortitude in the face of pressure. On more than one occasion,
Peter allowed his selfish interests and fear for personal safety to compromise vows of allegiance and fidelity. He was especially prone to
deny affiliation with those he loved if the appearance of his affiliation might implicate him. Peter was known to cave under pressure.

How can professionals stand their ground under pressure? First, you must anticipate. Develop the mindset that it's only a matter of time before you will be pressured to compromise. Second, you must be prepared. Consider appropriate responses to coercion and temptation *before* they occur. One helpful strategy to prepare is *behavioral rehearsal*. Practice exactly what you might say. That way you might avoid finding yourself dumbfounded like Arthur. Third, you must never lose sight of your purpose, your moral obligations, and the ethical standards you have pledged to uphold. Fourth, you must be humble. It's true. Pride does come before a fall. Fifth, you must cultivate a healthy support system. When temptation knocks on your door, you need people in your corner, people whom you can turn to, people who can help you to do what is right.

Key Components

- *Expect temptation to compromise your ethical commitments.*
- *Prepare for temptation and coercion by knowing your weak spots.*
- *Construct an excellent support system and seek consultation when temptation calls.*
- *Humble yourself and remember that moral frailty is part of the human condition.*

13
Do Not Be a Hypocrite

Amos was an opportunist, your friend one day and a backstabber the next, changing up when he came across chances to advance his career. As assistant vice president of human resources, Amos was delegated the task of developing and implementing employee assistance programs. He focused on personal counseling, substance abuse treatment, colleague mentoring and support, and professional ethics. His boss was Frieda, a vice president. When Frieda was assigned to a critical project for the corporation, Amos could see the handwriting on the wall. He knew that Frieda was having serious personal problems. She was going through an ugly divorce, and the toll dampened her attitude at work, interfered with her overall performance, and caused her to give the project much less attention than it required. Although Amos had been a friend and sometimes confidant, although Frieda had been an important mentor to him, and although he considered himself loyal, he sabotaged Frieda by curtailing his own efforts with the project, allowing her to fail miserably in the process. To add insult to injury, Frieda was "let go," and he was offered her job. Frieda knew the score, and Amos' conscience never allowed him to fully enjoy his promotion.

Imagine you are at a theater on Broadway eagerly awaiting the start of the play. After the lights dim and curtains open, you intently watch the performance of the actors. You see them laughing, crying, gibing each other, singing, dancing, and generally flaunting their acting wares. You are watching them put on a show. As someone who is there to be entertained, you are fully aware that the activity on stage is pretense, intended to give the illusion of real life.

Are you an actor in real life? What are you like when no one is looking? Do you behave the same way in public as you do in private? Do you change your behavior when you are in the company of people you respect? Is your behavior dictated by principle or by convenience? In short, are you a hypocrite?

Hypocrisy, derived from the Greek *hypokrisis,* connotes the ideas of playacting and unprincipled action. The real-life behavior of the hypocrite is a pretense, an act propelled by insincere motives. The surface behavior is designed to conceal, disguise, misrepresent, or even contradict the real motivations of the hypocrite. On this thought, poet and literary critic T. S. Eliot warns: "There is no greater treason than to do the right deed for the wrong reason." In contradiction to the socially accepted rule of pretense for a stage performance, the expected social norm in real life is sincerity. For instance, although we might disagree with their ideas, we generally respect people who practice what they preach and preach what they practice.

The consequence of hypocrisy is inconsistency. Hypocrites change their behavior, depending on the manipulative advantage they perceive to be gained in a situation. Hypocrites tailor their professional behavior to maximize their own personal gratification; they are fundamentally self-serving.

Key Components

- *Maintain consistency in behavior across contexts and relationships.*
- *Avoid pretense and practice transparency.*
- *Pay attention to internal moral distress, and seek to understand the source.*

2

Doing No Harm

Matters of Nonmaleficence

The Hippocratic oath enjoins physicians to "abstain from whatever is harmful or mischievous." Traditionally considered a rite of passage for doctors, the oath generally is attributed to Hippocrates, the father of medicine. So too must all professionals work to prevent harm to those they serve. This obligation applies to both active intent and harm resulting from negligence. The ethical professional remains vigilant to potential harm and makes every necessary effort to avoid or minimize damage. Consider nonmaleficence—the act of doing no harm—to be a minimal but fundamental moral expectation.

Key elements in this chapter include remaining alert to evidence of negative outcomes, resisting coercion, maintaining role boundaries, and remaining alert to the lure of sex, money, prestige, and power. Ethical professionals refuse to exploit others and resist efforts by others to misuse their work. Finally, ethical professionals make arrangements for their incapacity or death as a way of caring for those who might be impacted by this change.

14
Be Vigilant for Negative Outcomes

Dr. Henry H. Bennefield, a renowned classics professor, was delighted and humbled to be appointed provost at his university. Although he was a brilliant scholar, Dr. Bennefield struggled when it came to managing confrontation. For much of his adult life, he had been a conflict avoider, feeling anxious at the first sign of disagreement and hoping "everything would just work out." During his first year as provost, Dr. Bennefield had to contend with several volatile faculty issues. For instance, the dean of one college proposed a policy that would seriously harm the financial footing of the remaining six colleges. A senior male faculty member was accused by more than one female colleague of sexual harassment, and the board of trustees wanted to freeze faculty salaries and the hiring of full-time professors. On each occasion, Dr. Bennefield adopted his standard ostrich response—figuratively burying his head in the sand, hoping the situation would just calm down. But tempers flared, resentments mounted, and several deans and faculty members began to show signs of serious emotional distress. Only then did Dr. Bennefield finally realize his leadership style was counterproductive. He immediately sought coaching and leadership consultation. Although it was not easy for him, he learned to become assertive and proactive as a way of preventing harm to those he had pledged to serve. The university's faculty noticed the change and responded with gratitude and increased loyalty.

Ponder the successful efforts of one historical figure in his quest to stop negative outcomes. In 1847, Hungarian obstetrician Ignaz Semmelweiss, who became known as the "savior of mothers," made a discovery that dramatically reduced mortality rates among women during childbirth. The problem of higher mortality rates among women in hospital wards as compared with those of women in midwife wards perplexed him. Determined to solve this mystery, Semmelweiss eventually discovered the fatal but invisible puerperal infection, known then as "childbed fever." Physicians and medical students unwittingly were transmitting germs to patients simply because hand-washing and disinfection techniques were not part of protocol in hospitals of the day. Semmelweiss immediately ordered

physicians to begin washing their hands with a chlorinated-lime solution before each examination.

Although nineteenth-century medical practices seem archaic
when measured against the standards of modern-day medicine, Semmelweiss's discovery reminds us that even professionals who have the
best of intentions can inflict harm; good intentions are not always
good enough (Ridley, 2005). Harmful client outcomes may arise
from malicious intent, or more simply, misguided practice. Frequent
negative outcomes or those likely to harm others should trigger ex-
peditious attention. Are these outcomes connected to inexperience,
incompetence, or carelessness? If you were under scrutiny, would a
panel of your peers agree that you did everything in your power to
anticipate and avert such harmful results?

Professionals should work diligently to prevent harm to anyone
with whom they work. Preventing harm demands thoughtful evaluation of how things might go wrong and earnest effort to minimize
negative outcomes. When professionals see a co-worker in harm's
way, they act decisively; otherwise they run the risk of witnessing
harmful outcomes that may easily overshadow benign intentions.
The damage may be physical, psychological, social, or financial.

Professional ethics demand more than good intention: The most
important criteria for determining the appropriateness of professional behavior lies in its consequences. Of course, we cannot and
should not relegate ourselves to the self-serving philosophy that the
"end justifies the means." Unscrupulous action is never justifiable and
should not be tolerated even when there is the potential to achieve
the desired outcomes.

Like Semmelweiss, each professional must be vigilant for negative
outcomes—results that indicate our services are creating adverse or
damaging consequences for those we presume to help. From time to
time, ask yourself a simple question: Do my actions result in positive
or negative outcomes? Obviously, the answers are not always clear
cut, given the mix of dynamics in the workplace and the complexity
of interactions among people. Yet, in many instances, taking the time
to be vigilant can make all the difference.

Key Components

- *Anticipate and prevent harm to others whenever possible.*
- *Demonstrate a logical process for evaluating your professional outcomes.*
- *Respond immediately to minimize harm or repair damage when a client reports a negative outcome.*
- *Recognize that good intentions must be supported by good outcomes.*

15
Resist Coercion

Nothing in Roderick's experience prepared him for that hair-raising day in May. As a relatively junior air-traffic controller, Roderick had a sterling record of performance on the job. He was rapidly headed for a promotion. On a particularly busy May afternoon, at the height of business-travel rush hour, the airport experienced a near collision on a runway controlled by Roderick. Although the fault clearly lay with one of the pilots who had misidentified the correct runway on approach, Roderick was stricken by an awareness of what might have happened had he not detected the problem quickly, sounded the alarm, and instructed the pilot to take evasive action. But Roderick soon discovered that the near miss was the least of his problems. Abiding by protocol, Roderick completed a detailed incident report that same day. Yet his supervisor disputed several details and suggested the near miss was not nearly as close as Roderick had reported. She quietly asked him to rewrite the report, hinting that the airport really didn't need the extra scrutiny the report would trigger. He double-checked his figures and tried to consult with a couple of other controllers. He was certain of his estimates, and many of the numbers were recorded in a database. However, his colleagues strangely were mum, obviously not wanting to get involved. In spite of serious discomfort, subtle hostility from his supervisor, and even fear for his career, Roderick stuck to his initial report.

In a field of electrical current, a resistor is an entity that slows down or totally obstructs the flow of electricity. To effectively impede the electrical current, the force of a resistor must be more powerful than the force of the electrical energy. Regardless of its size or constitution, a successful resistor must be capable of impeding the free flow of electrons from one area of the circuit to their intended destination.

In human interactions, we often think of resistance as something negative, something that impedes constructive change. But picture this: Instead of electricity flowing through a circuit, imagine a coercive force, a dangerous agenda, or a conniving plan rushing through your professional setting. Will you have the grit and fortitude to slow it down or stop it altogether? Will you resist, or will you acquiesce? Failure to resist may have dire consequences—both for those you serve and for your own moral health.

We all are coerced at times during our careers. We are coerced when someone—often a power holder or someone with positional authority—marshals force or intimidation. The person attempts to coerce us into compliance. Sometimes coercion is overt and direct. You may be browbeaten, bullied, or threatened. Sometimes coercion is covert, subtle, and indirect. A colleague might state in no uncertain terms that you would be wise to participate in covering up the facts, or a boss might insinuate that your employment hinges on bending the rules. You might be excluded socially or labeled a "whistle-blower" for not participating in the cover-up.

These are only a few of the strategies that you might witness or actually have experienced. But coercion by any other name is still coercion. Whether overt or covert, the intent behind coercion is to force you into behavior unbecoming of an ethical professional. The dubious behavior may involve an unethical act or a transgression by omission—looking the other way when you should be acting as a resistor.

What happens when professionals fail to resist coercion? Sometimes lives are lost. On January 28, 1986, the space shuttle *Challenger* exploded just after liftoff, killing an entire crew of talented astronauts. A subsequent investigation revealed that several flight engineers had serious misgivings about the launch and the effect of the unusually cold weather on several key pieces of equipment. Feeling public and financial pressure to stick to the launch schedule, NASA officials effectively silenced the few engineers who initially went against the grain. Several had recommended aborting the launch.

Slowly, many of these professionals capitulated and fell silent. They became ineffective resistors.

Anticipation is the best counter to coercion. Nothing compares to readying yourself mentally, refusing to be taken off guard, and having the courage to withstand coercion's force. Preparation is the second line of offense in countering coercion. Discuss the problem with trusted colleagues and friends. Find out how others have handled their own bouts with coercion. Develop a mental script for responding to the inevitable coercive encounter.

Key Components

- *Actively resist efforts to coerce you to comply with unethical or unlawful practices.*
- *Seek supportive consultation from trusted colleagues when coerced.*
- *Be vigilant to both overt and subtle varieties of coercion.*
- *Remember that resisting coercion is a necessary method of avoiding harm.*

16
Do Not Blur Roles

Aziz had been a judge in family court for several years. Experience had taught him to "stay in his lane," as he put it. By this he meant stick to your job, stay within your professional role, and lower the chances of getting frustrated, making those in the courtroom confused, or engaging in judicial malpractice. This wisdom had come through difficult experience. Early in his judgeship, Aziz had often taken it upon himself to counsel parents in child-rearing techniques and speculate about the psychological impairment of a plaintiff or defendant, and once he had ordered a single mom to take her children to church. After some powerfully negative reactions from citizens, some formal complaints, and more than one warning from his supervisor, Aziz realized that nothing in his training or job description authorized him to practice amateur psychology or psychiatry, and that blurring his professional role as judge with that of father and parishioner simply was not appropriate. As a result of this jolt, Aziz

made a commitment to be careful and operate only within the accepted
boundaries of his profession—a family court judge. He exercised judicial
wisdom and applied relevant law carefully; and when the situation
called for it, he made appropriate referrals for mental health evaluations,
classes on parenting skills, and community support services—often con-
nected with local churches.

Baseball offers a good example of the importance of well-articulated roles. Every baseball team has nine positions. Each position is endowed with a clearly defined set of responsibilities, and players bring to each position a unique set of skills. On successful baseball teams, players stay within their roles. They know that overstepping their roles and straying into another player's position can have dire consequences. When players blur their roles, they quickly undermine the team's unity, productivity, and morale. In essence, the word *team* looses its meaning. In this context, nine players may be on the field, but the team is missing in action.

Like the governing organization for baseball, most professions clearly delineate appropriate roles for their members. *Roles* entail the kinds of practices or patterns of behavior expected of persons inhabiting a profession. They are determined by the functions and responsibilities of professionals. Whether you are a doctor or nurse, professor or student, manager or secretary, admiral or lieutenant, mayor or city council member, priest or parishioner, or coach or player, fulfilling your role is critical to the success of your organization.

Ethical professionals show great caution when it comes to blurring roles. There are both individual and organizational reasons for this caution. Seasoned professionals understand that by taking on more than one role with a client, consumer, or student, the professional is escalating the risk of losing objectivity and exploiting or harming the person served. So, when professionals add a business, social, romantic, or other role to an existing professional relationship, they may be less effective, and the client could be harmed. Naïve, inexperienced, or exploitive professionals are most likely to blur roles with those they serve.

Sometimes professionals employed by organizations are unclear about some aspect of their role-set, especially those roles that relate to organizational norms. This is *role ambiguity*. Professionals experiencing role ambiguity cannot easily gauge what roles are expected, what roles are appropriate, or perhaps how their performance will be evaluated. In some instances, professionals find that the role expectations communicated by an organization or client are simply inappropriate. In other instances, professionals may be obligated to provide services outside their role-set or may find that these expectations are at odds with the ethical standards of their profession. Alternatively, organizational expectations may place professionals in direct conflict with each other. This is *role conflict*. If you are experiencing role conflict, take this action: Ask your supervisor for clarification. Be prepared to make suggestions, and above all, refuse to operate outside your boundaries of competence, refuse to undermine other professionals, and refuse to blur roles with clients in a way that could be confusing, harmful, or exploitive.

Ethical professionals understand that blurred roles do not serve the interests of clients or their organizations. They accept responsibility for trying to remove the blur—both the blur within a role-set and the blur between role-sets. To these professionals, tolerating blur is tantamount to promoting chaos, and chaos is a definite script for self-defeat.

Key Components

- *Clearly consider and communicate your role with each client and consumer.*
- *Do not enter into secondary roles with clients without first seeking consultation and considering the risk of exploitation or harm.*
- *Remember that blurred roles can undermine your effectiveness and create conflict with clients and other professionals.*
- *Seek consultation before adding an additional role to an existing professional relationship.*

17
Beware of the Power of Sex

Rev. Michael Stevens was a dynamic youth pastor. The high school students at North Hills Community Church thought he was cool, someone who could relate to their generation. Parents were enamored of his positive influence on their teenagers. Within two years of his joining the church's staff, the youth ministry skyrocketed from about a dozen kids to more than 100. Like any 27-year-old, single male, Pastor Michael, as he was affectionately called, also had vibrant hormones. Still, Michael had no problem maintaining professionalism, not until Michal, a very mature and very attractive high school senior, developed a crush on him. Michal was tantalized by Pastor Michael's energy and charisma, the sincerity of his concern for youths in the church, and even the identical pronunciation of their first names. At every possible opportunity, she volunteered to assist in projects related to the ministry. One evening, after everyone else had gone home, Pastor Michael found himself alone with Michal in the church parking lot. Although his thoughts and impulses were erotic, he had the presence of mind to behave appriately and keep clear boundaries. However, when he went home that night, he was greatly disturbed and restless. He tossed and turned all night. The next day he called his best friend from seminary, confided in him about the situation, and asked for his support. Pastor Michael recognized his need for help in handling the unspoken but live dynamics between Michal and him. With his friend's assistance, he was able to put into action a plan of accountability.

Riveting sex scandals in modern times have flooded the airways and new media: Bill Clinton and Monica Lewinsky in the White House, Eliot Spitzer and Client Nine in the New York State government, Kobe Bryant and a groupie in basketball, priests in the Catholic Church, Mary Kay Letourneau and a minor in a public school, cadets in the military. These highly publicized instances of sexual impropriety are just the tip of the iceberg.

Sexuality is integral to humanity. With few exceptions, human beings have sexual feelings. These feelings often motivate sexual engagement and connection with another person. Except for cases of physical or emotional disability, all of us have the capacity to engage in sexual behavior. Finding yourself attracted sexually to another person is undeniably human. And considering that we spend most of our waking hours each week at work, it should come as no surprise that we can feel sexual attraction to co-workers or clients. Sexual attraction, to be sure, is not unethical. But ignoring the power of sex, acting on impulse, exploiting our professional position for sexual gratification, or otherwise compromising professionalism does constitute an ethical problem.

Unwanted sexual advances may be interpreted as disrespect, exploitation, or sexual harassment. In many professions such as law, psychology, and medicine, there are clear-cut ethical prohibitions against becoming romantically or sexually involved with clients. The ethical standards are intended to prevent professionals from compromising the value of professional relationships and from harming clients—even if the professionals' behaviors are underscored by benign motives. Although such prohibitions may not be equally iron-clad in all professions, we recommend extreme caution, concerted prudence, and thorough consultation should sexual attraction begin to change your thinking or behavior relative to someone you serve professionally. Professionals who are comparatively immature, lacking in self-awareness, or feeling entitled or impulsive may be at risk for ethical transgressions related to sex.

Handling sexual attractions responsibly should be the commitment of all professionals. Here are several guiding principles designed to assist you in fulfilling this commitment. First, be self-aware. The purpose of self-awareness is to overcome any tendency to deny or even lie about your real feelings, emotions, and desires. Once you acknowledge the truth about your romantic attractions or sexual feelings, you can make better-informed decisions.

Second, professionals need to accept their sexuality. Professionals never should consider themselves immune to sexual attraction. The irony would lie not in finding themselves attracted to someone but in never finding themselves attracted to anyone. Third, professionals should get consultation from trusted colleagues when sexual feelings threaten to diminish the quality of their services or lead them to cross professional boundaries with a client or customer. When—not if—

you become aware of strong feelings, turn to a friend or colleague who can give honest feedback and provide emotional support. The consultation should result in a plan of action that helps the professional avoid acting irresponsibly. Fourth, anticipate sexual attraction. Sooner or later, most professionals will be attracted to someone, or someone will be attracted to them. The attraction should not take you off guard. Have a plan in place for getting consultation. Develop sensitivity for the types of clients or other people that trigger your emotional or physical interest. Be prepared to respond professionally—even when doing so runs counter to powerful desires and wishes.

Key Components

- *Accept your own humanity, including your sexual feelings.*
- *Recognize that attraction to clients, co-workers, students, and others you serve is not unusual.*
- *Understand that acting on sexual feelings with any one you serve poses real danger to the professional relationship and the individual.*
- *Anticipate sexual attraction and have a plan in place for responding professionally.*
- *Seek consultation from a trusted colleague when sexual feelings threaten to compromise your professional judgment.*

18
Beware of the Power of Money

Camille's podiatry practice was solid, if not exceptionally lucrative. She enjoyed her work and had a particular niche in the geriatric community. Camille was pleasantly surprised when a large national sports medicine chain moved into her community and invited her to a meeting with the director over a sumptuous lunch. Because Camille did not have a specialty in sports-related injuries, she was interested to learn that the new sports medicine practice would compensate her for referrals of athletes—particularly high school students—who might benefit from sports rehabilitation services. Camille agreed, and within the first six months of this arrangement, she was startled to discover that her income had increased significantly due to rather large "referral fees" the practice reimbursed her for. In addition, Camille was treated to frequent meals out and even a weekend getaway in a mountain ski condo owned by the sports medicine company. Camille's practice was fine until she mentioned her new income to a colleague who immediately identified her "fees" as kickbacks and questioned whether they were ethical. After some soul-searching, Camille was forced to admit that her referral fees were hidden from her clients and that she had referred several patients whose need for sports medicine services was marginal at best. In the end, Camille decided she no longer could accept referral fees and made referrals only when they were clearly in her clients' best interests.

As a medium of exchange, money can be acquired and used in numerous ways. People can acquire money honestly through hard work, saving, living frugally, investing, receiving an inheritance, or even winning the lottery. They can employ money for benign and even altruistic purposes such as paying bills, putting kids through college, saving for retirement, helping neighbors, or supporting charitable organizations. But money can also be acquired by theft, extortion, blackmail, fraud, or acting on illegal insider information. And once obtained, money can be used for a seemingly endless array of nefarious purposes. Although money is itself merely a symbol—alone it is neither good nor bad—it holds the power to corrupt even the most well-intended professional.

Dishonesty in the acquisition and use of money is age old. In the Bible, Judas betrayed Jesus for 30 pieces of silver. Slavery was once the foundation of a profitable economy in the United States. Evangelist Jim Baker misappropriated millions of dollars from innocent supporters of his ministry. The Enron scandal exposed multimillion-dollar corruption in corporate America. These events seem to ring consistent with the biblical saying "For the love of money is the root of all evil" (I Tim. 6:10).

As professionals, we engage clients in *fiduciary* relationships, relationships rooted in trust that imply that the professional must always act with the clients' best interests at heart. Because misunderstandings or outright misbehavior underlie a disproportionate number of ethical and legal complaints against professionals, they must take extra care to be thoroughly transparent regarding all financial arrangements bearing on their work. Make fees, billing matters, and anything else relevant to money clear from the outset. It is especially important to avoid kickbacks or hidden fees for referring clients to other providers or organizations. These arrangements usually are hidden and may hinder a professional's objectivity.

Never forget that money is a powerful *reinforcer*. A reinforcer increases the chances that a behavior that precedes it will reoccur. It should come as no surprise that when professionals are reinforced financially for cheating, misappropriating funds, engaging in insurance fraud, or accepting kickbacks, these behaviors are likely to reoccur. Unlike *primary reinforcers* such as food and water, *secondary reinforcers* such as money can feed a seemingly insatiable appetite.

Early in their careers, professionals need to develop a healthy perspective on money. Certainly, they should seek financial security. Certainly, it is appropriate that they accumulate wealth as they capitalize on fair and ethical financial opportunities. But all of us must resist the temptation to define our personal worth in terms of financial power. We never must attempt to accumulate wealth at the expense of investing in character. We always must treat money as a means to an end but never as an end itself. Developing this perspective early in one's professional career may save considerable angst.

Great ethical peril lies in store for professionals who have unchecked struggles with money matters. You are vulnerable to financial impropriety. If the struggle comes from the condition of your personal finances, find a financial adviser. You need help in establishing a plan to put your finances in order. If the struggle emanates from simple greed, find a professional counselor or religious leader. You need help in overcoming your money addiction.

Key Components

- *Be alert to the powerful—though subtle—temptation of money.*
- *Accept fiduciary responsibility for any client you serve.*

- *Make all your financial arrangements transparent from the start.*
- *Avoid kickbacks or other arrangements that might diminish your objectivity.*
- *Seek professional consultation for personal financial problems.*

19
Beware of the Power of Prestige

A successful life coach and executive consultant, Sally was thrilled when asked to launch her own daily television show. Charismatic, articulate, and experienced, she soon had a loyal following and developed a reputation for offering thoughtful career and personal advice to busy professionals. As her reputation grew, Sally was hardly aware of certain changes in her own behavior. For instance, she became more outrageous in her advice to clients—often trying to achieve a laugh from the audience. She meted out advice with very little assessment or careful consideration of clients' specific circumstances, and she became less judicious when making blanket statements about human behavior—many of which were not well supported by existing research. Things came to a head when Sally took her show "live" to the home of a recently fired and publicly disgraced CEO. Without getting permission or the CEO's consent, she knocked on the door of his home with cameras rolling, offering an "intervention" to get him back on track. After a painful lawsuit and an ethics complaint from her professional organization, Sally was forced to honestly confront the allure that publicity and prestige held for her. She decided to quit the television show and go back to serving private clients.

What motivates you? Are you motivated by money, self-satisfaction, great achievements, the pursuit of excellence, or perhaps knowing that you contributed to society? Is your primary source of motivation internal or external? What really drives your behavior? How do you determine personal success? Only you really can answer these questions, and your answers can shed light on one aspect of ethical vulnerability.

Everyone, to some degree, is motivated by the need for recognition, affirmation, and validation. Prominent psychologist Abraham

Maslow took up this theme in 1943 when he presented his *theory of human motivation*. He postulated that people have five basic needs—physiological, safety, belonging, esteem, and self-actualization. The esteem need, which is of interest here, has two versions. In the higher form of self-esteem, people have the need for self-respect, which includes feelings of confidence, competence, achievement, independence, and mastery. In the lower form of self-esteem, people have the need for the respect of others, status, fame, glory, recognition, and reputation.

The higher form of self-esteem is internally motivated. While affirmation from others is appreciated, people at this level are self-confident and are content with the internal satisfaction associated with achievement. On the other hand, the lower form of self-esteem is externally driven. People who operate primarily at this level seek public fame or glory, an outcome that is dependent on what others think and say about them. Certainly, all of us would like to be held in high regard, and none of us want to be viewed with disdain or disinterest.

As you now may surmise, professionals with needs for the lower form of self-esteem are most vulnerable to the power of prestige. Wishing for recognition, adulation, and affirmation, these professionals may elevate their needs above the interests of clients. The process may take place without these professionals' conscious awareness. A powerful hunger for attention or an exaggerated sense of self-importance is dangerous for the same two reasons as an unchecked desire for money. First, the need cannot be satiated. The more prestige these professionals achieve, the more they want, resulting in an endless cycle of prestige-seeking behavior. Second, people will do almost anything to attain the prestige they so desperately seek. Here is where they are vulnerable to ethically inappropriate behavior.

Although needs for prestige may be expressed out loud or carefully shrouded, professionals whose esteem rides on external reinforcement may stop at nothing in their attempts to gain recognition or achieve acclaim. Cutting corners, cheating, manipulating, playing favorites, going back on one's word, and stabbing a colleague in the back may all be viable options for these people.

Prestige-seeking behaviors often reveal personal and spiritual discontent. Meeting prestige needs can take precedent over claiming higher ethical ground in one's professional life.

Key Components

- *Recognize and take ownership of your needs for adulation and recognition.*
- *Appreciate the danger of seeking prestige at the expense of those you serve.*
- *Explore the reasons for frequent prestige-seeking and get professional assistance if this behavior interferes with professional obligations.*

20
Do Not Abuse Power

Cordell's meteoric rise to the position of senior manager in an international construction firm had surprised even him. He was ambitious, smart, motivated, and loyal to the company that had given him his first job as an engineer right out of college. But his inexperience and lack of character were evident when it came time for his first opportunity to offer promotions to several junior engineers. Although Cordell oversaw a division comprising numerous subspecialties within engineering, it soon became apparent that the electrical engineers—Cordell's own specialty— mostly were the ones getting promotions. Further, if an engineer of any specialty happened to be female and attractive, there was a very good chance that she would be promoted, even over more professionally qualified and better-performing males. When two of his subordinates drew his attention to the perception that attractive women and electrical engineers were getting unfair advantage in career development, Cordell reacted angrily and threatened to demote them. Finally, the vice president—noticing that several engineers in key specialties other than electrical were leaving the company—pulled Cordell aside, confronted his bald abuses of power, and stripped him of the authority to make promo-

tion decisions independently. This was a painful experience but Cordell finally did "get it." He mellowed, becoming considerably more sensitive to the ease with which power could be abused.

Imagine living in a world without power. Nothing would work. Nothing would be accomplished. No progress could be made. Remember when your car battery went dead, when you were typing on your computer and a power outage struck your neighborhood, or when your physical strength gave way and you could not finish a project? And who can forget the failure of power grids in various geographical regions? These stark realities remind us of the necessity of power for a well-functioning and productive society.

Similarly, power operates in professional relationships. Some experts describe all human relationships as power relationships. The issue is not whether power exists in relationships, but whether power is used for constructive ends. Most would agree that in the right hands, power enables much good. But when power is applied wrongfully, when power harms or diminishes others, an *abuse of power* has occurred. There are several important points to make about abuses of power.

First, abuses of power occur in the widest range of relationships and contexts. Actually, potential abuses of power are too many to name. Making unreasonable demands on subordinates, playing people against each other, making arbitrary decisions, coercing clients to go along with our recommendations, withholding rewards, making false accusations, and playing cut-throat office politics are just a smattering of the numerous ways professionals abuse their power.

Second, abuses of power are self-serving. Psychiatrist Len Sperry makes the point that professionals who abuse their power do so in the service of their own needs and interests (2007). These interests may be emotional, sexual, or financial. Whatever the source of the abusers' needs and interests, the wrongdoing occurs at someone else's expense. And make no mistake: All human beings can be tempted to use power for personal gratification. Perhaps this is why English historian Lord Acton famously warned, *Power tends to corrupt and absolute power corrupts absolutely.*

Third, abuses of power often are processes and not single, discrete events. While it certainly is true that some abuses of power involve a spontaneous action, most are better described as an unfolding story of escalating advantage taking. The process may begin when a professional uses his or her position to gratify a need or recognizes an opportunity to reap some gain. In some cases, abuses of power are carefully orchestrated. The person is deliberate and calculating in planning the abuse. In other cases, a professional may have poor self-awareness or unconscious needs that find more subtle expression in manipulation or coercion.

Fourth, abuses of power are self-reinforcing and desensitizing. When abusive professionals achieve their anticipated results, they are more likely to abuse again; emotional, financial, or sexual gratification are highly reinforcing. Like stepping onto a slippery slope, initially abusing power desensitizes the professional to unethical behavior, thereby increasing the probability of more egregious abuses.

Here is a final admonition: Nearly every professional-client relationship involves some power imbalance. The professional is the identified expert. Clients, patients, customers, students, and other subordinates typically defer to your expertise, and more often than not will have great difficulty saying no. It is always the professional's duty to recognize power imbalances and act in a way that safeguards the less powerful party's best interests.

Key Components

- *Remind yourself often that you hold a power advantage in many relationships.*
- *Remember that power imbalances create risk for exploitation and abuse.*
- *Avoid taking advantage of or coercing a subordinate in any way.*
- *Accept the fact that power can corrupt you; you are human.*
- *Be aware of the intoxicating effects of power and the slippery slope of abuse.*

21
Never Exploit People

All that seemed to matter to Coach Gail Mallory was winning the NCAA championship and establishing a legacy like Pat Summit and Geno Auriemma. As head of women's basketball at Alton State University, she savored becoming the center of media attention. Within three years, she turned a nondescript, losing basketball team into a national powerhouse and sure bet to appear in the Final Four. To be certain, she relished the media attention lavished on her at this midsize university. But behind the scenes of this storied program, something scathing was brewing. Coach Mallory had become a different person, increasingly harsh, demanding of her players, insensitive, and bordering on cruel. For Coach Mallory, it was all about winning—winning at any cost. The players could not talk to her about anything but basketball. When personal problems arose, she told them "Get over it." When minor injuries became apparent, she told them, "Play through it." Things fell apart two weeks before March Madness. Anika Monroe, an all-American point guard and candidate for National Player of the Year, stormed into the coach's office and announced that she was quitting the team. "If I have to be your toy, I don't need basketball that much." Startled and shaken to her senses, Coach Mallory called an emergency team meeting, allowed the players to express their grievances, and promised to be more considerate. Although real change required a slow and deliberate process, this confrontation marked a dawning awareness of how she had shamelessly exploited the young women who called her "Coach."

In 1932, the U.S. Public Health Service commenced a study to observe the long-term effects of untreated syphilis on a group of unsuspecting African American men. These semiliterate men were deceived and exploited. Although they were promised free treatment for their condition as compensation for participation in the study, the men were given ineffective substances such as "spring water" and aspirin. The scientists even convinced local physicians not to treat the men. The study continued for 40 years until at long last it was exposed by the news media. By then, many of the participants were deceased or suffering painful and preventable deaths. In reaction to the

Tuskegee study and other abuses in biomedical and behavioral research, Congress commissioned the Belmont Report (U.S. Government, 1979), which created strict protections of research participants' rights. This report came too late for the men of Tuskegee.

Exploitation is a travesty of the highest order. In *The Elements of Mentoring*, we described exploitation this way:

> Exploitation is the selfish use of someone else for one's own ends or profit. It translates into treating people as objects rather than as human beings. Exploitation also involves taking an unfair advantage. A person in a position of relative power and authority exploits a person who is in a power-down, dependent, or vulnerable position. (Johnson & Ridley, 2004)

Exploitation reveals itself in several telltale signs. These include the use of deception and manipulation, the abuse of power, and the mistreatment of a person who is comparatively vulnerable in relation to the professional. Entering into multiple roles with a client (e.g., professional, social, business, and romantic) also heightens risk of exploitation. When a professional charges a wealthy client an exorbitant fee, accepts lavish gifts as a form of barter, or uses a client's vulnerability to meet emotional or sexual needs, exploitation has occurred. Professionals who deny the impact of their own position and power are more likely to exploit those they supposedly serve.

Make no mistake. Exploitation relegates unfairly used individuals to the status of inanimate objects. *Inanimate* means that which is lifeless and lacks the power of movement. We use inanimate objects for purposes and without consideration of the psychological or spiritual consequences, for they are lifeless. Furthermore, exploitation can manifest itself in the widest range of behaviors—some overt and some covert. Overt exploitation, like threatening to fire impoverished employees if they do not accept substandard wages, is easy to detect. Covert exploitation, like encouraging clients to offer public testimonials of one's services or using a client to meet one's emotional needs, is more insidious.

To minimize the risk of exploitation in any relationship, here are some questions to ask: How will the person benefit from my action? How might the person be harmed by my action? If the person understood the consequences of my action, would he or she find it acceptable? Have I taken the person's own concerns into consideration? The fundamental question is this: Would a jury of your professional colleagues—fully apprised of your behaviors and the client's needs—agree that you acted exclusively with the client's best interests at heart? If not, address at once those areas in which you may be taking unfair advantage.

Key Components

- *Avoid selfish use of another person for your own benefit.*
- *Be sensitive to the power imbalance in professional relationships and refuse to ignore clients' power disadvantage.*
- *Reject arrangements, policies, or relationships that create even the appearance of exploitation.*
- *Always ask how any professional action will benefit those you serve.*

22
Prevent the Misuse of Your Work

Ecstatic about her new discovery, Jennifer was anxious to present her research at the Annual Meeting of the American Sociological Association. A second-year doctoral student and the protégé of a prominent social scientist, she could not wait to share the findings with her adviser and mentor, Dr. Yu-Lin Chan. The discovery was based on a large data set that Dr. Chan had collected over a period of several years. Unknowingly, Jennifer had reached a conclusion based on a statistical fallacy called "data dredging." The statistically significant results of her secondary data analysis most likely were spurious given the very large number of variables that she had analyzed. Although the results were accurate, the interpretation was flawed. It certainly was difficult to burst Jennifer's bubble, but Dr. Chan decided to use this as a teaching opportunity. Even though she initially considered letting the problem go and letting Jennifer move ahead with a publication based on the erroneous interpretation—another publication would certainly have helped Dr. Chan's career—she understood that being complicit in this activity would make her a party to scientific misconduct.

In the United States, *espionage* is defined as the act of obtaining, delivering, transmitting, communicating, or receiving information about the national defense with an intent, or reason to believe that there is one, to use the information to the injury of the United States or to the advantage of any foreign nation. Although espionage may be among the most outrageous examples of misuse of one's work, at some point every professional will discover that some of his or her work has been used inappropriately.

At some point, your professional advice, research data, published work, or public statements will be applied in a way that you did not intend, possibly in a way that can cause harm to you or others. Another party may misuse your work deliberately or may misquote or misapply your work accidentally. Although this misuse may not be illegal, it can constitute a genuine ethical problem. Misuse may diminish the public's trust in your work or cast a negative light on your entire profession. It also may lead persons to make misguided decisions and thereby cause harm. As the professional involved, you may or may not become aware of the misuse.

Professionals have an ethical obligation to prevent the misuse of their work whenever possible. There are several ways that you might consider decreasing the chance that someone will use your work in a harmful or spurious manner. First, whenever you present or publish findings or conclusions based on your work, thoroughly explain the limitations and caveats so that others are not tempted to draw grandiose or unfounded conclusions. Second, to the extent feasible, remain vigilant for evidence that your work is being misapplied or misused by consumers or other professionals. Third, when evidence of misuse becomes apparent, immediately investigate the claim, and if it is valid, bring the problem to the attention of the person or organization responsible for the misuse. Fourth, request tangible evidence of compliance with your requests to correct errors related to your work or cease and desist unfounded or inaccurate references to your work. Finally, if the offending party is not willing to make corrections and retractions as necessary to protect the public or prevent harm, consider formal intervention in the form of an ethical complaint or legal action.

Key Components

- *Present your work in such a way that misinterpretation or misuse would be very difficult.*
- *Remain vigilant for evidence that your work is being misused by frequently reviewing relevant forums, publications, and media.*
- *Respond immediately to evidence of misuse by requesting retractions or corrections.*
- *Publicly correct inaccurate statements about your work.*
- *File formal grievances or complaints when needed to protect the public from the misuse of your work.*

23
Plan for Illness, Incapacity, and Death

The law practice of Albert Lee was a fixture on the Upper East Side of Manhattan. He had faithfully served the legal needs of three generations of New York City families and took pride in the fact that he was often an adopted member of many of these extended families. If not entirely surprised, the Manhattan community was deeply saddened by Albert's passing at the age of 78. He had remained active in his practice until the end. Many of his clients were quite upset and alarmed at the news and wondered how complicated it would be for them to retrieve important documents and to transfer their legal work to other attorneys. Each of them was pleasantly surprised to receive both a certified letter and a phone call the following business day. The letter was from Albert. He had prepared it in the weeks before his death, and it had been mailed by his estate on his death. The letters thanked them for their patronage, explained in detail the current status of their account and their legal circumstances, and clearly outlined the plan for transferring their legal files to one of several highly recommended attorneys—the choice was theirs. The phone call was from one of Albert's assistants, reiterating the plan, asking if there were questions, and initiating the process of confidential transfer to any attorney the client preferred. All of Albert's clients later reported a deep sense of gratitude that even in death their attorney was taking good care of them.

Conscientious people take careful steps to ready themselves for both inevitable and unanticipated life events. In our personal lives, we take out insurance in anticipation of potential illness, accidents, fire, and even death. We prepare for retirement by investing in 401(k)s, annuities, and employer retirement programs. We try to protect our children by instructing them in how to react to strangers, and we seek to educate them by establishing a college fund. We join AAA in the event that our vehicle becomes disabled while we travel. As in our personal lives, we should leave nothing to chance in our professional lives.

Most ethics codes enjoin professionals to plan for their own illness, incapacity, or death. Part of serving others professionally is the need to arrange for the continued protection of their best interests in the event that we no longer can serve them. In spite of our herculean efforts to deny this truth, every professional one day will retire or die—most hoping that retirement comes first. And there will be career-altering events: You may become sick, incapacitated, or have a family crisis that requires you to take some time off from work. While we cannot anticipate or plan for every conceivable event that lies ahead, we can prepare for the possibility of a prolonged illness and for the inevitability of death.

Here are some ethical imperatives bearing on this element of professional practice. First, plan for your absence or death from the start. Be sure that clients know that a plan exists and even provide the names of those colleagues who will cover for you in advance— perhaps during the informed consent process. Second, make arrangements with trusted colleagues who agree to step in and provide continuity for your clients should this be necessary. Be sure these colleagues have an up-to-date plan for taking custody of your records, protecting confidentiality, notifying your clients expeditiously, and providing continuous care. Third, if an illness, progressive condition, or pending retirement is involved, give clients plenty of time to absorb and prepare for the end. Allow them ample opportunity to say good-bye, achieve closure, and transfer to another professional. Finally, consider a professional will. Consult an attorney to draft a specific plan for its execution in the event of your incapacity or death.

Planning for your own absence is a hallmark behavior of the ethical professional. It is an ethical imperative that you not *abandon* your clients. Provide the same level of thoughtful consideration for death or prolonged absence that you provided in the best days of your practice. Preparation builds *spirit decor*. It shows your goodwill. Preparation eases transitions on both practical and emotional levels and helps organizations maintain efficiency.

Key Components

- *Prevent abandonment of and harm to clients by planning for their care in your absence.*
- *Inform your clients about who will cover for you should you no longer be able to provide professional services.*
- *Make detailed arrangements with colleagues and consider drafting a professional will for execution in the case of your incapacity or death.*
- *Do not deny the inevitability of your own retirement or death; plan carefully.*

3

According Dignity

Matters of Respect

Professionals respect the dignity and worth of all people. In our professional work, all of us must protect the welfare of those we serve and make sure that we avoid infringing on other people's freedoms. We accord dignity when we support each person's right to privacy and self-determination. We further accord dignity when we communicate that each client and consumer we encounter has inherent worth. All human beings are valuable without having to prove their value. Respectful professionals are particularly prone to accord dignity to others regardless of race, ethnicity, nationality, gender, religion, sexual orientation, and any other human difference.

In this chapter, we cover those elements of ethics with greatest bearing on the virtue of respect. Ethical professionals honor human differences. They respect values. They behave respectfully and professionally in every context. In addition, they protect the privacy of other people, and refuse to undermine them. Finally, they confront irregularities when they arise.

24

Honor Human Differences—All of Them

The superintendent faced a difficult task. In response to a court ruling, he would be responsible for admitting the first class of women to a prestigious all-male military college. He faced resistance from almost all sides. Alumni, students, and even some professors showed intense hostility, creating an unwelcoming and chilly environment for the first class of women. Initially, there was demeaning name-calling, ridicule, insults, and, sometimes, expletives. Stereotypes were used to exclude women from clubs and traditions, and small groups of male students circulated "underground" publications disparaging their new female classmates. The superintendent wasted no time tackling this challenge head on. He addressed the college's student body, warmly welcomed the women, and laid out his zero-tolerance policy, which included dire consequences for anyone who participated in harassment. He reminded students of their obligations to support the constitution and the rights of all citizens. In the weeks that followed, he expelled several male students for harassment or abuse. He hired more female instructors and elevated a female professor to the position of dean of students. He arranged for several high-profile women speakers to visit campus and began upgrading the athletic facilities to ensure that female students had the same resources as their male counterparts. In the end, all stakeholders in the college were forced to confront their stereotypes, dispel their fears about women hurting the college, and learn to appreciate the rich contributions both genders bring to the campus environment.

Anthropologists Clyde Kluckhohn and Henry Murray penned a widely quoted dictum. A paraphrase of what they said is that each person is in certain respects: (a) like all other people, (b) like some other people, and (c) like no other people. Their take-home point is just as instructive today as it was a half century ago. All human beings are unique regardless of their race, culture, ethnicity, gender, sexual orientation, religious affiliation, or any other group characteristic. In addition to their membership in the human race and their affiliation with a reference group, they have their individuality. Using this observation as a starting point, we can derive from it a timeless ethical principle. People should be appreciated and honored for their uniqueness. Indeed, honoring human differences is the ultimate criterion for according dignity.

Ethical professionals *actively* consider and honor the cultural backgrounds and values of those they serve. They work at developing general knowledge about and sensitivity to the many groups with which they work. They avoid assigning pathologic labels to the behaviors of people from different cultures, and they do not tolerate demeaning or disparaging comments, humor, or behavior in the workplace. Ethical professionals treat everyone with respect and dignity. If they are uncertain about the meaning of certain aspects of someone's culture and understanding of those aspects is crucial to the working relationship or provision of service, they respectfully ask questions. Preferences for appointment times, modes of communication, meeting arrangements, and specific professional services are some areas that might warrant investigation. After gaining new insight, culturally sensitive professionals may need to make adjustments in their own thinking and behavior to facilitate a healthy working relationship.

Look at human differences from yet another angle. Psychologist Carl Rogers coined the concept *internal frame of reference* in 1961 to help us appreciate how we might better understand people. Through his many years of psychological practice, he concluded that one of the necessary ingredients for effectively helping clients is empathic understanding. Empathy is the capacity of therapists to understand and tune into their clients' internal frame of reference, which consists of their feelings, emotions, attitudes, and outlook on life. It should be of interest that Rogers sometimes used the term *envelop* to capture the idea of the internal frame of reference being circumscribed. Rogers believed that clients are most likely to change when they perceive that a therapist begins to see the world through their eyes, through their psychological lenses. As clients experience the therapist's empathic understanding, they experience the freedom to be authentic about the insides of their envelopes, lower their defenses, and explore new ways of approaching life. This line of thinking posed a challenge to the well-entrenched psychoanalytical point of view. Instead of therapists single-handedly interpreting the inner world of clients, Rogers argued that clients themselves were the best source for interpreting their inner worlds.

Stereotyping is the real danger in discounting human differences. A stereotype basically is a label. It is a mental shortcut that allows us to oversimplify and make rapid generalizations about individuals or groups. Once we have a stereotype firmly fixed in our minds, we are unlikely to attempt to gather more information and test it for its accuracy. It might surprise you to know that there is a "kernel of truth" in some stereotypes. But for the most part, they are inaccurate. Over time, stereotypes decrease our empathy, erode our sensitivity, and prevent us from really understanding each person we encounter as an individual.

The ethical response to stereotyping is to challenge the idea, gather more information about the person or group, and put the stereotype to the test. Then quash disrespectful comments or attitudes when they emerge from colleagues or subordinates. Quash them in yourself as well. Steadily increase your own knowledge and cultural sensitivity by seeking out cross-cultural experiences.

Key Components

- *Deliberately consider the cultural identities of those with whom you work.*
- *Be vigilant to stereotypes in yourself and others.*
- *Consider ways to honor the culturally based needs and preferences of those you serve.*
- *Celebrate differences, and demonstrate an interest in understanding culturally different clients.*
- *Do not tolerate harassment or discrimination related to cultural differences.*

25
Respect Values

A church's board of elders sent out an official call for a new pastor. The new pastor would replace a beloved incumbent pastor who was to retire after 28 years of service. After seven months of searching and interviewing, they found their man. Rev. Rowland Mansfield had a dynamic vision for the church, convincing the elders that he could help the church grow, reach out to the surrounding community, and implement innovative ministries that appealed to younger generations. Because the church had stagnated and the number of congregants was down, initial enthusiasm for Mansfield ran very high. Unfortunately, after only 12 months on the job, Mansfield recognized that the elders wanted him to bring in new people and make the church more contemporary, but without changing many cherished traditions, liturgies, and practices. While Mansfield strongly valued evangelism and cutting-edge programming, the congregation strongly valued tradition and conservative approaches to worship and outreach. When, during a meeting with two senior pastors in his district, Mansfield described his congregants as "backward, rigid, and resistant to change," his colleagues immediately confronted him for his lack of sensitivity and respect for his flock's essential values. Mansfield came to understand that only by first communicating respect for the values of his congregants would he earn enough credibility to help them begin the slow process of change. This insight marked a positive turning point in the development of the church.

Everyone harbors values. Values are beliefs, philosophies, and convictions about self, others, the world, and how one ought to live. Values reflect what really matters to us. In our society, for instance, many people value achievement, independence, freedom of speech, religious freedom, material possessions, security, and self-determination. Not everyone holds to these values or places the same degree of importance on them, but they are prevalent in our culture. In addition to societal values, individuals hold personal values, and these vary from person to person. One person values a structured work setting; someone else, an unstructured one. One person values fame and celebrity; another person values obscurity and privacy.

Values are powerful. They shape our lives, underlie our behavior, and inform our decisions and life choices. Some of our values are explicit. We state them openly and confidently. Because they are not tangible—you can't see, touch, or hear them—a lot of values are implicit. Although we cling to them dearly, we do not make them clear to ourselves or others. Implicit values provide fertile soil for conflict and for ethical problems. They may be difficult to decipher and are prone to ambiguity or confusion.

Focused exclusively on technical competence, some professionals overlook how values play a critical role in professional relationships. In many instances, they may acknowledge and honor the values that others hold dear. They may seek to understand others' commitments, ideas, and beliefs, while they avoid prematurely judging people. But they may not understand that respecting another person's values does not have to imply agreement. Some professionals assume that they must endorse values—either their own or other people's—without careful analysis. However, in their efforts to remain unbiased and respectful, they erroneously equate *respect* with *uncritical acceptance* (Ridley, Ethington, & Heppner, 2007). Although it is imperative to respect the values of clients and colleagues, it is equally important to critically examine how values create conflict or promote unethical behavior.

Ethical professionals should actively explore their own values as well. They should try to figure out the origins of their primary values and consider how consistent their primary values are with the ethical principles and standards of their profession. If they find inconsistencies, they should determine why and honestly consider how this incongruence may impact their professional work and those they serve.

Now here is a final word of warning: Beware of the danger of *values imposition* on clients, students, and others over whom you hold a power advantage. Research shows that in professional relationships, clients often begin a subtle process of shifting their own values to match those of a respected professional (Beutler and Bergen, 1991). Deliberate efforts to impose one's values on another—particularly when these values are religiously or culturally significant—are probably unethical and potentially harmful. Consider what may happen in counseling and psychotherapy when the therapist is from an individualistic culture and the client is from a collectivist culture. The therapist may misjudge the client's strong affiliation with family as codependency, a reflection of the therapist's cultural value of rugged individualism. Recognize with humility that some of those you serve will slowly shift their own values to more closely align with yours. This can be an unnerving burden. Take this responsibility seriously.

Key Components

- *Respect others' values—especially those that diverge from your own.*
- *Explore and understand your own primary values commitments and remain sensitive to potential values conflicts when serving others.*
- *Recognize the power you wield to influence values in those you serve; avoid values imposition.*

26
Behave Professionally at All Times

Sonya was not one to shrink from a tough duty. A relatively young high school mathematics teacher, she was known as a difficult but eminently fair teacher who had a knack for helping turn around kids who had behavior problems. When the district superintendent needed a mathematics department head for a new alternative high school for troubled teens, Sonya immediately came to mind. She responded enthusiastically to the challenge and, to no one's surprise, was soon instrumental in helping many of the school's "lost causes" achieve academic success. Sonya's students were particularly intrigued by her genuine interest in their cultural experiences and her consistently dignified, respectful treatment of them. But Sonya discovered that her impact on students was multiplied manifold due to her encounters with them outside school. In their small town, she encountered students in the grocery store, on the softball diamond, at community events, and even at church. Based on some of their comments and inferences, it became apparent to Sonya that the students took notice of the consistency between her demeanor in the classroom and during off-hours. They held her in high regard because she accorded them the same dignity and modeled the same virtues (e.g., integrity, hard work, caring) that she espoused during the week.

A famous televangelist is discovered with a prostitute just months after publicly exposing and humiliating two colleagues for sexual indiscretions. A former Major League Baseball "player of the year" testifies before Congress on the dangers of steroid use—denying his own involvement—and tests positive himself during the ensuing baseball season. A decorated NASA astronaut goes on an impulsive cross-country trip for the purpose of killing a romantic rival. A congressman resigns in shame after sending sexually inappropriate messages to teenage assistants. Do you notice a theme emerging in these real-life scenarios? Through acts of personal indiscretion, highly respected individuals bring dishonor to themselves and their profession writ large. In each case, the public's faith in the profession is damaged.

Don't kid yourself. Your ethical obligations do not stop when you exit the building at the end of the workday. Being an ethical professional requires more than following the rules of your profession from 8 to 5. It entails your comportment, your mindset, and all of your personal choices, not just those made while you are at work. Behaving ethically as a professional—using the language of author Robert Bellah and his associates—is a "lifestyle style of life" (Bellah et al., 2007). At all times, it means a commitment to the ideals of your profession whether or not you physically are on the job. Furthermore, it means responsibilities and obligations that extend beyond the needs, interests, and benefits of the individual sitting across from you in the office.

All of us have the right to privacy. We all need time outside our professional roles to recharge our human batteries, relax, enjoy entertainment, and engage in personal reflection. But when our off-hours attitudes or behaviors undermine our credibility and expose inconsistencies, it's time to regroup. Estimating the personal damage for your indiscretions is usually difficult. But estimating the damage to stakeholders in your profession when your personal transgressions mar its reputation is impossible. Being a professional makes it obligatory to behave professionally at all times and with propriety in all situations.

Key Components

- *Be ethical in both your professional and personal life.*

- *Accept that professionals are highly visible and that with visibility come certain obligations.*
- *Establish a pattern of consistent behavior.*
- *Understand that unprofessional or unethical behavior will damage your profession and undermine your colleagues.*

27
Protect Privacy

Reginald enjoyed an excellent reputation as an executive coach. Organizations often referred to him managers whose interpersonal, emotional, or social skills were lacking and interfering with their performance. Reginald's interventions often straddled the fence between psychotherapy and executive skill development. His rate of success kept his waiting list lengthy. Because the referring organizations paid his fees, extending the coaching relationship beyond a few months often required a formal request. The request typically was made to the vice president for human resources. Cautious to protect confidentiality, Reginald always was careful to secure a signed release of information and informed consent agreement from his clients before having these conversations. However, Reginald also was conscientious about protecting his clients' privacy. This meant that when human resources personnel went on what Reginald called "fishing expeditions," he had to have safeguards. Occasionally, he would get subtle queries about a client's substance use, childhood history, sexual orientation, or feelings about specific leaders in the company. When these queries came, Reginald was quick to redirect them to the key reasons for referral, the key foci of coaching, and the prognosis for change.

In certain professions, the nature of the professional-client relationship mandates the protection of confidential information. Law and psychology are two professions in which client confidentiality is protected. In chapter 1, we noted that professionals have a fundamental ethical, and often legal, obligation to protect confidential information disclosed to them in the course of their work.

Most of us understand the importance of *confidentiality* and the premise on which it is based—assurance that clients can self-disclose without the threat of their disclosures being used to cause them harm. Ethical professionals protect confidentiality in their reports, presentations, and consultations. However, many professionals do not understand the distinction between confidentiality and *privacy*. For many of them, there is no distinction, or the distinction is blurred. Understanding the distinction between these two concepts can inform professionals' ethical conduct and help them circumvent ethical and legal pitfalls.

Privacy is the basic right of individuals to decide how much of their personal information they wish to have shared with other people. It may be defined as freedom from intrusion into one's private life. Privacy covers a wide range of personal information, but it essentially concerns anything that is not relevant to individuals' successful performance in the workplace. Privacy and confidentiality share the interest of protecting people. However, privacy goes beyond ethics because private information has legal protection.

How do professionals err when it comes to privacy? First, they may succumb to the human temptation to discuss juicy details about a client with friends or family members ("you won't believe this but . . ."). Second, when making an appropriate disclosure, such as when a release of information has been signed by the client, the professional may exceed the level of detail required to convey the essential point or conclusion (e.g., mentioning a client's substance abuse history, sexual orientation, or marital status when this information is irrelevant to the purpose of the disclosure). Finally, professionals sometimes intrude on client privacy by making inquires or asking questions that fundamentally are voyeuristic. The information is not salient to the professional's task or role (e.g., seeking detail about a client's sex life or financial situation).

The concept of privacy is granted by the Fourth, Fifth, and Fifteenth Amendments to the U.S. Constitution. It is a right that is due everyone, not just clients of professionals who adhere to a code of ethics. Privacy is essential to ensuring human dignity and the freedom of self-determination (Koocher & Keith-Spiegel, 1998). Take note of these amendments and protect clients' privacy by collecting only information germane to your professional work.

When a client gives written consent for you to speak with other parties, reveal only the data necessary to achieve the professional purpose.

Key Components

- *Protect the privacy of those you work with professionally.*
- *Never request information that is merely interesting or tangential to your role.*
- *When it is appropriate to discuss a client outside the professional-client relationship—that is, when a signed release of information exists—disclose only the information that serves the interest of the client.*
- *Recognize that privacy is protected by the Constitution.*

28
Never Undermine Other People

An established tax attorney, Karen had developed a prosperous law practice in her community. When a pair of lawyers fresh from law school—a husband-and-wife team—moved to her area and also launched a tax law practice, she was overcome by anger and felt threatened by the new competition. Her initial impulse was to protect "her turf" and look for opportunities to scuttle the couple's new business venture. In a more sober moment, however, she realized that her attitude flew in the face of everything she believed about professionalism. She knew that undermining her new colleagues was not the thing to do. Instead, she called to welcome them to the community and invited them to a gathering with several other lawyers in the city. She referred a few clients to them from her own waiting list and endeavored to be as cordial as possible. When a colleague informed Karen that one of these new lawyers was giving erroneous tax advice in a convoluted area of state tax law—advice that could potentially lead to a malpractice claim—Karen called this competitor, explained what she had heard, kindly clarified the tax code, and offered to serve as a consultant should this ever be helpful. The new lawyer was immensely relieved to have averted a major problem. Ten years later, after a serious illness caused Karen to take an extended leave of absence, it was this same lawyer who single-handedly jump-started Karen's practice with a giant influx of referrals.

In the world of athletics, the gold standard is the *level playing field*. Everyone who plays or observes sports is indoctrinated with two time-honored rules: Play fair, and don't cheat. In theory, these rules make it possible for every athlete, every coach, every team, and every franchise to have an equal opportunity to compete and win. In the interest of fair play, no one is supposed to have an unfair advantage or unfair disadvantage. The gold standard is undermined when these rules are broken. Athletes betting on games, athletes taking performance-enhancing drugs, officials accepting bribes, and coaches engaging in recruiting violations make it impossible for all parties to have an equal opportunity to compete and win.

In the realm of ethics for professionals, the gold standard also is fairness. According dignity demands that we protect the rights and welfare of the people and communities we serve. Professionals must be sensitive especially to the protection of vulnerable populations—those most at risk of being exploited by unfair practices. All members of society are supposed to have an equal opportunity to perform to the best of their ability and succeed in their work. As in athletics, no one should have an unfair advantage or unfair disadvantage to succeed.

But fairness is compromised when professionals undermine other people, whether these individuals are consumers, peers, subordinates, or superiors. In a free marketplace, there is a place for healthy competition. Most people want to be successful. As the saying goes, "May the best man win." But when does a fair advantage degenerate into an unfair advantage? When does a superior talent, strategy, or work ethic give way to undermining? Here are some of the most common forms of undermining in professional life:

- Plagiarizing or otherwise taking credit for someone else's work.
- Soliciting a person whom you know or suspect is currently served by another professional.

- Providing competitors with erroneous information that is likely to undermine their decision making.
- Spreading gossip in the professional community or making a bogus complaint about another professional merely to undermine and create a relative advantage.
- Violating accepted professional norms or standards as a means of undercutting other professionals.

Playing the game of undermining is a slippery slope. When deception and manipulation become commonplace and using them to get an unfair advantage is the goal, the ethical moorings of professionals are all but lost. Deception and manipulation are diametrically opposed to fair practices, according dignity, and staking out the high ground on which professionals ought to stand.

Key Components

- *Pursue fairness in all of your professional activities.*
- *Reject opportunities to achieve competitive advantage through deception or manipulation.*
- *Never undermine colleagues through rumor or efforts to lure away their clients.*
- *Recognize that fair practices pay off manifold in the long run.*

29
Confront Irregularities

It was billed as collaboration. Early-stage plans already were starting to be made. Everyone who had a stake in the development—the city fathers, business leaders, developers, and investors—was at the table. Everyone was there, that is, except the people who would be adversely affected by the ambitious plans—the poor residents who were about to be displaced from the section of the city. Sure, there would be provisions for these residents' relocation. Sure, money would be set aside for the expense involved. Sure, the project would spur economic development in the city.

*After the residents got wind of the first meetings, several of the more
vocal ones organized a protest. Robert L. Goldstein, a prominent defense
attorney in a nearby community, heard from a friend about the plight of
the residents. He offered to take their case pro bono. His basic challenge
to the City Planning Commission was this: Billing the development
project as collaboration was inconsistent with the behavior of the leaders
who were moving the project forward. How can the city claim collaboration when one group of important stakeholders is given no voice in the
formulation of the plans? The confrontation yielded a positive outcome.
Representatives of the community were included in the planning of the
development. Their concerns about how relocation would proceed were
given considerable attention.*

We can cull some lessons about how to deal with irregularities
from some wise people. "All that is necessary for the triumph of evil
is for good men to do nothing." These sobering words, attributed to
British statesman Edmund Burke, leave an indelible imprint on our
collective psyche. German theologian Martin Luther stood his
ground and defied practices he saw as unscrupulous in the church.
His defiance still echoes today: "Here I stand. I can do no other."
Donning the courage of conviction, these men exemplified uncommon personal ethics by openly confronting irregularities. We should
listen to their words and heed their example.

Martin Porter (2002) makes an astute observation of Burke's
classic quote. Much of history is shaped by silence, he asserts, and
bystanders are the unidentified perpetrators of and collaborators in
wrongdoing. By doing nothing, they demonstrate their complicity.
As Dr. Martin Luther King Jr. poignantly stated, "In the end, we
will remember not the words of our enemies, but the silence of our
friends" (Bainton, 1995). According dignity and respect is easy
when there is little cost involved or no price to be paid. But taking
the ethical high road and demanding that each person's dignity be
respected when we ourselves may suffer harsh consequences for
our insistence is another matter indeed. Then it may be not so
easy.

Confrontation is the deliberate identification and clarification of
perceived irregularities, inconsistencies, or discrepancies in the be-

havior of another person or in the collective behavior of a group or organization. The purpose of confrontation is to pinpoint and correct the irregularities, inconsistencies, or discrepancies—particularly those that may harm others—and then facilitate the person or social unit's movement in the direction of ethically appropriate behavior.

Why don't many professionals confront obvious ethical problems? There are at least two key reasons for inaction in the face of glaring irregularity. First, some professionals, who otherwise are highly competent and assertive, are afraid to speak out against things they know to be wrong. They fear the consequences of speaking out, of how they might be adversely affected. Their fears are legion and may include rejection, ostracism, retaliation, loss of status, financial penalty, and numerous other social and psychological consequences. Unlike Martin Luther, the pious theologian, or Dr. Martin Luther King Jr., the prominent civil rights leader, they lack the courage of conviction. Second, some professionals do not understand the purpose of confrontation. They have the misguided idea that any form of confrontation amounts to a vicious personal attack. Professionals who harbor this idea may treat confrontation like a weapon to figuratively annihilate colleagues. But real confrontation is constructive, not destructive. Confrontation—when done well—consists of two phases: *critical examination* and *supportive challenge* (Ridley, Ethington, & Heppner, 2007).

In the first stage of confrontation, the goal is to determine whether or not confronted individuals (a) actually behave in an ethically inappropriate manner and (b) are aware of the inappropriateness of their conduct. The worst thing to do is presume that the behavior is inappropriate or that individuals who should be confronted recognize the problems with their behavior. Neither may be correct. If the behavior in question is found to be ethically inappropriate, the professional initiating the confrontation needs to move to the second stage of the intervention.

In the second stage of confrontation, the goal is to help individuals change their irregular and potentially harmful behavior. This stage may include a variety of strategies such as helping them explore their personal values, helping them see the adverse consequences of their behavior, and modeling for them ethically appropriate behavior. Correction always is the ideal outcome in this stage. Only when efforts at correction fail is more drastic action required (e.g., filing an ethics complaint). Here are some practical guidelines to assist you in confronting:

- Accept confrontation as a necessary ethical practice.
- Recognize that the need to confront may come at any time.
- Establish a constructive relationship with colleagues so that in the event of confrontation trust already exists.
- Time the confrontation so that it is neither premature nor unnecessarily postponed.
- Anticipate resistance to confrontation.
- Provide guidance and constructive feedback to colleagues as they strive to be ethically appropriate.

Confrontation is seldom fun. For many people, confronting someone is a disconcerting, gut-wrenching experience. However, that is beside the point. Confronting irregularities that may signify unethical or illegal behavior is a defining ethical obligation. Once admitted to your professional guild, you owe it to the public, your clients, your colleagues, and to your profession writ large to calmly explore and, when warranted, assertively challenge inappropriate practices.

Key Components

- *Do not turn a blind eye to evidence of malpractice or wrongdoing.*
- *Collegially explore and address questionable practices with colleagues or other professionals.*
- *Be assertive in confronting clear evidence of inappropriate behavior; your own discomfort must not create inaction.*
- *If informal confrontation is not successful, take additional steps as necessary to address the concern.*

4

Benefiting Others

Matters of Beneficence

Professionals work hard to benefit those with whom they work. In all of their professional interactions, they seek to safeguard individuals' welfare and rights and, as previously discussed, take considerable care to prevent harm—deliberate or incidental. Professionals should weigh all of their decisions in light of their potential benefit to others.

In this chapter of *The Elements of Ethics,* we summarize those elements of professionalism that serve to further the well-being of those with whom we work. Ethical professionals demonstrate flexibility and collaboration in their work—particularly when misunderstanding or conflict arises. They clarify expectations, communicate clearly, and achieve an ongoing sense of informed consent in their work. Ethical professionals make sure they are competent. They operate only within the boundary of their established competence and make referrals when new demands or requests exceed their capacity to perform competently. When making referrals, professionals are selective, careful to ensure the credibility and competence of those to whom they send their clients. Always having an open mind and knowing the limits of their competence, ethical professionals eschew defensiveness and seek consultation and second opinions whenever these might enhance their effectiveness.

Beneficence carries another implication: As human beings, professionals clearly have their own needs and desires. It is neither necessary nor realistic for them to deny these needs. In fact, needs such as emotional self-care and enjoyment of one's work should receive high priority as long as they result in beneficence and do not cause harm to others. The keys are for professionals to (1) identify their needs, (2) differentiate their needs from the needs and wishes of the people they serve, and (3) thoughtfully consider which of their needs are appropriate to meet through their professional work and which are not (Behnke, 2006).

30
Establish Win-Win Solutions

Martin knew he had his work cut out for him when he became an area director for sales in a major pharmaceutical company. The area directors had become acrimonious and fiercely competitive with one another. They intruded on one another's territories, undermined one another's success, and withheld information that might have boosted a colleague's sales figures. As a result, the company's profits suffered. Determined not to succumb to this toxic atmosphere, Martin began communicating regularly and cordially with the other directors, routinely passing on promising sales leads in colleagues' territories, and cheering them on when things went well. Although viewed with suspicion at first, Martin's approach started to change the culture. Several of the directors warmed up to his ideas about sales strategies as they saw firsthand the benefits of collaboration. When Martin's sales escalated on advice and referrals from colleagues, he devised a method of sharing the sales credit. His colleagues reciprocated, and soon the entire atmosphere among area directors had shifted. Martin's win-win approach was credited with a marked increase in sales throughout the company.

Bertrand Russell, a noted philosopher, once predicted that the only possible redemption for humankind would be cooperation; and

Albert Einstein, a highly acclaimed scientist, recognized that "every kind of peaceful cooperation among men is primarily based on mutual trust." These great men extolled the virtue of cooperation. In the face of compelling reasons to fight, ethical professionals seek cooperation, connection, and mutually beneficial outcomes.

All you have to do is serve on an ethics committee in any profession. You will be astonished at the number of otherwise bright and capable professionals who become the subject of ethics complaints because they polarize relationships, intensify conflicts, and lose sight of the fundamental obligation to honor the best interests of others. In the service of exacting revenge, defending a fragile ego, or collecting a simple fee, professionals engage in the most egregious of behaviors. They stop speaking to their clients, withhold vital records, engage in public shouting matches, make slanderous statements, ridicule people they do not like, and triangulate colleagues. When blind self-interest or bald egotism governs their behavior, they allow reason to go out the window, and fail to honor the principle of beneficence.

Polarizing relationships with clients, colleagues, trainees, and others is never beneficial. Conflicted, fractured relationships never serve the best interests of the people professionals are obligated to serve. Ethical professionals are ever mindful of the need to collaborate with colleagues and clients as a way of ensuring the best outcome from their relationships.

Finding win-win solutions to problems, the antithesis of polarization, may require professionals to make sacrifices. Sometimes, in the midst of sharply divided perspectives and high emotions, yielding some ground on both sides of a disagreement may be the most prudent course of action. Ethical professionals may have to relinquish any "right" to place their interests first. For instance, the need to enjoy relationships with colleagues or clients and consumers may have to take second place to working out mutually beneficial solutions. The moment people step into a professional role and accept fiduciary responsibilities, they forego the right to always have the upper hand or make the professional relationship a battleground for their competitive instincts.

Here is a documented fact: Professionals who have higher levels of *emotional intelligence* are significantly more skilled in regulating their own feelings (e.g., anger) and channeling their energy into more cooperative ways of engaging and building trust, especially with difficult people (Goleman, 1995). Emotionally intelligent professionals can see beyond their immediate frustration precipitated by a client's behavior or a colleague's slight, and they appreciate the long-term benefits of mutual cordiality, kindness, and cooperation. It is of interest that emotionally intelligent parents do not rely on spanking as a primary parenting tool, and emotionally intelligent leaders are more likely to use affirmation than humiliation.

At one time or another, finding win-win solutions will be needed in every area of life and work. When obligations to our code of ethics appear to conflict directly with a law, regulation, or organizational demand, we make these conflicts known to all parties involved and then work diligently to find a mutually acceptable middle ground. When our interests are impacted negatively by a client's financial circumstances, we seek a reasonable solution—perhaps a revised fee structure—as a means of avoiding unhelpful conflict. When an unexpected windfall results from a collaborative venture, we consider the fairest approach to profit sharing.

Here is a final word about collaboration: Don't forget your obligation to assist struggling colleagues. How much better will it be for your impaired colleague, for his or her clients, and for the credibility of your profession if you lend a helping hand? You might offer your colleague assistance, support, and encouragement. Reporting impaired colleagues to a regulatory board should be the least desirable option. Taking care of colleagues in distress is a tangible manifestation of the golden rule: In your professional life, do unto clients, colleagues, students, and others as you would have them do unto you. Chances are they will respond in like fashion when there is an opportunity.

Key Components

- *Seek your clients' best interests first.*

- *Choose collaboration over competition with colleagues and clients.*
- *Find opportunities to be cordial and strengthen relationships.*
- *Assist colleagues and clients who are struggling.*

31
Obtain Informed Consent

As a nurse practitioner affiliated with a major university medical center, Donna occasionally irritated a few of the physicians and administrative staff with whom she worked in the oncology center. Donna's primary role involved commencing and monitoring patients' trials of experimental medications for cancer. Her colleagues' good-humored annoyance was caused when Donna would often run overtime with patients due to her scrupulous commitment to ensuring that they embarked on the medication trial "with eyes wide open." Even though patients were asked to read all the details of the treatment and the medication specifics before the first appointment, Donna insisted on taking time at the first meeting to ensure that each patient received a careful description of the medication; its expected benefits and side effects and potential risks; and alternative treatment options. She slowed down this process to be sure that patients fully understood the implications of proceeding and had ample opportunity to ask questions or clarify facts. Donna's patience and clear commitment to the informed consent process were secretly admired and respected by her "annoyed" colleagues and deeply appreciated by her patients.

It is difficult to safeguard the best interests of those you serve if they are unable to give consent for the service you provide. Respect for the rights, dignity, and autonomy of others necessitates obtaining informed consent from the individuals impacted by your service. Informed consent allows consumers to weigh the risks and benefits of participation in research or an intervention. It empowers them to make careful decisions about their own lives, helps protect them from harm, and helps enhance trust between the professional and the consumer.

Like many ethical standards, the imperative of informed consent emerged from some notable ethical transgressions. Consider the shocking case of Yale University researcher Stanley Milgram and his experiments on obedience to authority. Beginning in 1961, Milgram conducted a series of studies in which ordinary citizens were led to believe they were participating in a learning experiment. They were instructed to administer electric shocks to a "learner" each time he or she failed to respond with a correct answer to a memory test (Milgram, 1974). As the research participants administered shocks of steadily increasing voltage to screaming, pleading, and, eventually, silent "learners," many of them protested and became visibly distressed. When a researcher in a lab coat ordered the participants to continue, nearly two-thirds of them obeyed, inflicting what they believed were potentially lethal shocks to another human being. Although the shocks were not real and the "learners"—accomplices of Milgram—never experienced any harm, the experiment clearly caused significant emotional turmoil for some subjects. Had they been informed of the nature of the disturbing feelings they might encounter, many would have likely refused to participate.

How can you ensure that the consumers and clients with whom you work have full and accurate informed consent? Here are key questions relevant to any informed consent process: (1) What is the exact nature of the service you will provide? (2) Does the person have a right to decline participation? (3) What are the alternatives to the service you recommend? (4) What are the expected benefits and potential risks? (5) What are the financial arrangements and billing practices? (6) Are there any limits to confidentiality or could there ever be a time when you might disclose information about individuals without their consent? (7) Are there any emergency procedures or avenues for contacting you that consumers should know about? Of course, the appropriate features of informed consent may change depending on the circumstances and nature of the professional relationship.

How much information must you share with a consumer in order to achieve adequate informed consent? Consider the *reasonable professional* standard: What would the typical person in your profession say? What is the standard of practice in your profession, and does this standard ensure that consumers have a clear understanding of the service and your business relationship? If you can not answer these questions in the affirmative, go beyond the prevailing standard. Remember that informed consent is both an ethical and legal obligation in many jurisdictions. You might be exposed to considerable liability if litigation ensues and no informed consent was secured or documented.

The failure to secure adequate informed consent may be caused by several common errors. First, too many professionals frame informed consent as an *event*—a onetime task to be completed at the outset of the relationship. This is a mistake. Informed consent is a process, an ongoing and open dialogue between the provider and consumer. Ethical professionals appreciate informed consent as an opportunity to inform and educate consumers while ensuring their full awareness of the implications of a service. This process must be rooted in good communication and clients' explicit understanding that professionals will keep them updated as circumstances, options, and recommendations change. Second, professionals who are hierarchical or paternalistic toward consumers may minimize their clients' need to know the details of the service rendered. This is the *professionals-always-know-best fallacy*. Finally, some professionals make little effort to secure informed consent from a legal guardian should the primary consumer be underage, medically impaired, or mentally challenged. They should understand this responsibility as obligatory.

Key Components

- *Respect your clients' right to autonomy, dignity, and self-determination.*
- *Conceptualize informed consent as a process, not an event.*
- *Ensure that consumers have full understanding of any service before you deliver it.*
- *Ask yourself what a reasonable professional in your field would consider adequate informed consent.*
- *Obtain informed consent in both verbal and written formats when possible.*

32
Clarify Expectations

An excellent teacher and active researcher, Chris was a very popular professor among undergraduates in management. Students often volunteered to work in Chris's research lab, hoping to gain valuable experience en route to graduate programs. Students whom Chris advised seemed to have better odds when it came to admission to competitive MBA programs. Chris had a humble appreciation of the exciting synergy and mutual benefit that came from having bright students assist him with research projects. He also appreciated the positive impact his advocacy could have on a student's subsequent career success. To ensure these mentoring relationships hummed along without misunderstanding or conflict, he was careful in clarifying his expectations of each new research assistant and each new advisee who was a major in the department. In exchange for research assistance and excellent work from students, Chris provided individual advising, weekly research supervision, and, subsequently, letters of recommendation to graduate schools or prospective employers. Students knew exactly what Chris expected and how he would evaluate them. Students overwhelmingly reported feeling "safe" and well supported in their relationships with him.

Here is a hard-learned nugget of ethical wisdom: Conflicting expectations cause angst. Clients and colleagues often become emotionally charged—most often hurt and then angry—when a professional fails to clarify expectations before plowing ahead. A significant number of ethical complaints and lawsuits could be averted if professionals simply took some time to make sure that, as the saying goes, *everyone is on the same page.* You will be on the same page with clients, customers, and colleagues when you obtain a mutual framing of the problems and set work parameters that are agreed on.

The great English poet Alexander Pope once opined, "Blessed is the man who expects nothing, for he shall never be disappointed." However, we know this saying does not apply to most people. Professionals and consumers hold myriad expectations—some obvious and some more subtle. They also have their fair share of disappointments. Therefore, the question is not, do we have expectations? but, do we share or at least appreciate one another's expectations for this relationship?

Think of the clarification of expectations as an extension of good informed consent. At the outset of a professional relationship, what can clients expect? How long will the relationship last, and how often will you meet? What is the macropurpose of the relationship, and what are the near-term goals? What will each party deliver in this exchange, and what does each party expect in return? Does each party agree to specific deadlines? Is an explicit agreement about the contours or boundaries of the relationship necessary? Are certain interactions or types of contact off limits? How do both parties anticipate terminating the relationship? When should termination take place?

Clarifying expectations is especially important in all professional roles in which you lead or supervise others. With the privilege of power comes a demand for clear communication about salient expectations. For instance, what are your performance expectations? What are the criteria by which subordinates will be evaluated? What is the process for decisions regarding promotion and salary increases? Here is the bottom line: Do those you lead know exactly what you expect? Do they clearly grasp the criteria you will use to evaluate performance? If not, it is time for clarification.

As a professional, your responsibility is to lead in clarifying expectations. Professionals who do not clarify expectations early on in relationships inadvertently are casting the die for later misunderstanding. It always is helpful to conceptualize expectation clarification as a process. In taking this approach, professionals occasionally can revisit expectations and ensure a shared vision about what each party will contribute to the relationship.

Finally, be transparent. All of us have expectations. The only question is whether you are thorough in revealing everything you expect of clients, subordinates, and colleagues. If you are not transparent, if your key expectations are not clearly spelled out, and if there are marked differences between what you and the people around you expect, then you are not fulfilling an important aspect of beneficence.

Ethical professionals seek clarity, congruence, and full disclosure in all settings and relationships.

Key Components

- *Be clear and transparent with regard to your expectations.*
- *Seek agreement on expectations between you and the people you serve.*
- *Make implicit expectations explicit.*
- *Take initiative to discuss and clarify expectations with others.*
- *Be sure that subordinates understand performance expectations.*

33
Make Sure You Are Competent

As one of the newest CPAs in the accounting firm, Tamar was a rising star. A graduate of an Ivy League MBA program and a very sharp junior accountant, she quickly earned the confidence of the firm's partners. At the end of her first year, Tamar was rewarded with a large bonus and was assigned to oversee the accounting for one of the firm's midsize clients. In a meeting with this company's vice presidents, it became clear that a pending merger and the planned sell-off of some major assets would have substantial and complicated tax implications. Tamar understood immediately that her lack of experience as an accountant and lack of expertise in tax law might seriously hamper the quality of her work with the company. She informed senior management that she wanted to bring in other experts from the accounting firm. They readily agreed and appreciated her integrity. Although her own supervisor at the accounting firm initially was surprised and annoyed at her request for consultation with more senior accountants, Tamar clarified in no uncertain terms that her first obligation was to the welfare of her clients. She would not allow her own inexperience to compromise the quality of the services they received.

Competence rests at the heart of professionalism. True professionals demonstrate marked skill and expertise in the practice of their vocation. Their honed skills and in-depth knowledge, in addition to impeccable character and commitment to a code of ethics, separate them from amateurs.

What is *competence*? Most of us intuitively recognize competence when we see it. *Competence* is best defined as having the necessary knowledge, abilities, skills, and values that enable professionals to reach their goals and achieve positive outcomes in their work. Competent professionals habitually and judiciously blend good technical knowledge and skill with effective communication, moral values, and empathic regard—all in the interest of beneficially serving their organizations and constituents. Although appropriate education and training are nearly always prerequisites for competent functioning, academic degrees and certifications can never guarantee that a professional is competent. Credentials do not necessarily equal competence.

Think of competence as an overarching capacity consisting of a set of *competencies*. Competencies are the specific techniques, skills, attitudes, or bits of knowledge that are integral to competence. Ethical professionals understand that microcompetencies are necessary but not sufficient. Competence is a deep and integrated structure requiring the professional to skillfully manage and integrate various virtues, abilities, attitudes, and focused skills (Wood & Power, 1987). It is the ability to think in terms of the macro, to seamlessly integrate and deploy these competencies at the right time and in the right dosages, and with the right touch, that makes a professional competent.

Here is the tricky part: Competence is fluid, not static. You may achieve competence at one point only to have it ebb over time should you fail to stay current in your field or allow your skills to rust. Personal crises, substance use, and other distractions can temporarily diminish competence. If competence exists on a continuum, you must take responsibility to know where you fall on the continuum. In determining whether you are competent, it is wise to consult with an experienced colleague in your field. Based on your training, education, experience, and performance, do other professionals consider you competent? Based on this consultation, would others agree that you are competent as a *general* practitioner of your profession, or do you have *specialty* competence in specific areas as well? Ethical professionals refuse to operate in any area outside their established competence. Here is a firm guideline: If you would be uncomfortable with colleagues knowing that you are offering a particular service or engaging in a specific professional practice, you could be bordering on incompetence.

So why do so many professionals exceed the limits of their established competence? Here are a few of the many reasons: Financial stress may cause professionals to operate beyond the scope of their training. Impatience may lure others to take shortcuts along the arduous path to accumulating the necessary education and experience. Of course, raw egotism may underlie some professionals' pursuit of high-profile work, regardless of its match with their credentials and competence. Some people just become indifferent, allowing staleness to set in and doing nothing to stay on the cutting edge.

Remember this advice: Becoming and staying competent is not simply about you. Competence is about beneficence and non-maleficence. Ensuring your own competence benefits those you serve, and it also protects them and minimizes potential harm. Ethical professionals refuse to accept referrals in areas in which they have not established competence. When working with clients or engaging in tasks that exceed their competence, they make this known to the parties involved, and then make appropriate referrals. They are tenacious in keeping themselves up-to-date, accurate, and relevant. Finally, in the interest of protecting the public, they take personal responsibility for collegially confronting incompetence in colleagues.

Key Components

- *Make sure that you are competent to practice in your field.*
- *Maintain competence through continued education and training.*
- *Refuse to operate outside the boundaries of your competence.*
- *Seek consultation from other experts before practicing in a new area.*
- *Firmly but collegially confront incompetence in colleagues.*

34
Communicate Clearly

A social science researcher with a small organizational consulting company, Jeremy was thorough in his approach to conducting large-scale survey research for various public entities. When he was given the assignment to conduct a census of homeless men and women in a large midwestern city, he set about creating a comprehensive yearlong study. His research involved three separate sweeps of the city to count the number of homeless. His quarterly report to city planners, following the second count in February, revealed a drop of 40 percent in the number of homeless persons on the street. A front-page story soon appeared in the city paper that featured a quote from the mayor explaining that recent research supported cutting funding for homeless agencies by 40 percent. Jeremy was mortified. He immediately contacted the city planner who commissioned the research, the mayor's office, and the newspaper reporter and explained to each of these entities that the 40 percent drop was attributable to the subfreezing temperatures. When data from homeless shelters were added, the total number of homeless in the city actually appeared to have increased slightly. These essential data had either been overlooked or ignored by the mayor's office. When this clarification ran in the next issue of the paper, Jeremy's supervisor received angry calls from the mayor's office and threats to terminate funding for the study. Jeremy was undeterred.

Irish poet William Butler Yeats said, "Think like a wise man but communicate in the language of the people." Perhaps nothing so quickly will undermine your good work as will poor communication. Even the most brilliant and talented professionals risk misunderstanding, relational carnage, and lawsuits when they fail at the task of communication.

We all know good communicators. Some professionals are naturally gifted in the art and technique of imparting information, ideas, and even emotions. They impress us with an intuitive ability to establish rapport with those they encounter. They calmly, carefully, and thoroughly convey essential information to consumers and colleagues. These professionals recognize that communication is a two-way street. Actively listening to and reflecting others' concerns is the first step to strengthening any relationship. Although good communication may be part intuitive ability, it also requires large helpings of hard work. Making sure those with whom we work understand what to expect from us and our services, the rationale for specific procedures, and their rights and service options should not be taken lightly. Excellent communication demands patience. Far too many busy professionals sacrifice thorough communication on the altar of overcommitment and harried schedules. Ensuring that consumers' questions are answered and anxieties quelled may occasionally take a larger slice of time and effort than planned. But it is always well worth the investment.

So why have we nested clear communication within the beneficence chapter? The answer is simple. Benefiting those who seek our services requires communication designed to further their interests. The ethical professional cares for others by providing timely feedback, sharing information in such a way that it is both comprehensible and useful, and taking time to ensure clarity in expectations. And there is more. Beneficence demands equal attention to squashing misunderstanding or misuse of one's work. Not only must professionals avoid deliberate miscommunication—ranging from overt fraud to subtle, misleading phrasing—they also must be on the lookout for malicious efforts by others to exploit or misconstrue their work. In these instances, ethical professionals make special effort to confront, clarify, or issue public corrections as necessary to promote accuracy and protect others.

In *Gift from the Sea* (1955), author Anne Morrow Lindbergh reflected that "good communication is as stimulating as black coffee and just as hard to sleep after." To this we might add that clear communication rests at the heart of ethical practice. Maintaining integrity and promoting the welfare of others demands attention to clarity in our words, as well as tenacious confrontation of misuse of our work.

Key Components

- *Take time to communicate clearly with those with whom you work.*

- *Never assume that others understand information you take for granted.*
- *Listen carefully to determine what you should clarify for others.*
- *Actively confront and correct any misunderstanding or misrepresentation of your work.*

35
Refer Cautiously

Lincoln was an associate pastor and a professional pastoral counselor in a thriving metropolitan church. Lincoln's exceptional counseling work and his thoroughgoing professionalism were highly respected among colleagues and clients. Attuned to his ethical responsibilities and primarily concerned with his clients' best interests, Lincoln frequently referred clients to psychiatrists (for medication evaluations), psychologists (for psychological evaluations), social workers (for family work and social services), and substance abuse treatment programs. In each of these categories, Lincoln had a very short list of professionals to whom he would refer. He listened carefully to colleagues and clients about their impressions of various professionals. He often would invite professionals new to the area to lunch. In addition to becoming acquainted with them, he wanted to ascertain if they were potential sources for referral. And he was particularly vigilant to any evidence of unethical practice or disrespect for his church members' religious faith. He liked to think that doing good reconnaissance was essential to making the right referrals. As a pastor, he was fond of saying, "A good shepherd won't send his sheep to the wolves."

Nobody is perfect. All of us harbor areas of relative weakness—zones in which we lack competence because of inexperience, lackluster training, or the degradation of skill due to neglect. Our ethical codes enjoin us to make referrals when our boundaries of competence are exceeded or various conflicts threaten to undermine the efficacy of our service. In these circumstances, the willingness to refer in order to safeguard the best interests of those with whom we work is indicative of genuine professionalism.

The question, then, is not simply whether or not to refer, but, how, when, and to whom shall I refer? Lets consider the *how* question first. Keep in mind that any referral should be for the sole purpose of protecting and benefiting your client. Remember, your clients hold less power in the relationship. They also may be in distress or weathering difficult circumstances. For these reasons, our clients are especially vulnerable to misunderstanding our motives for making a referral. They easily may feel rejected and abandoned. The ethical—and skillful—professional is attuned to these risks and takes care to explain the purpose and potential benefits of any referral. An effective referral requires a measure of emotional intelligence—empathic regard for clients, even those we no longer can serve. Patiently clarifying your ethical obligation to refer may be useful.

When should a referral be made? When your professional experience and competence is exceeded, when your own functioning is compromised by serious personal distress, when the relationship has become so strained or conflicted that you no longer can be an effective advocate for the person's best interests, when it becomes clear that special expertise is required, or when your work with the client has failed to yield any significant gain or improvement over time—these are the instances when it is right to make a referral. When is it considered unethical or unprofessional to refer someone? Referring a client the moment he or she runs out of health insurance, referring someone merely for the purpose of initiating a different kind of relationship (e.g., romantic, sexual), or referring merely because a client or consumer annoys you or raises questions about your services might be considered ethically questionable.

When it is clear that a referral is appropriate and when care has been given to framing the referral so that clients understand how the change will best serve their interests, professionals must ask the *to whom* question. The ethical obligation to protect one's clients and act with their best interests at heart extends to the referral process. Here are some key questions to ask yourself before making any referral: (1) Does the professional have demonstrated competence or expertise in the necessary domains of practice? (2) What is his or her track record of success with clients? (3) Has the professional established a reputation for thoroughgoing ethical behavior? (4) Are there any obvious conflicts of interests, or is there a preexisting relationship between the client and the professional?

Here is a final caveat: Avoid accepting any fee or *kickback* for making referrals. Although there is often an implicit culture of fee splitting or overt remuneration for providing client referrals, such arrangements are rarely transparent to clients and rarely in their best interests. The promise of financial reward for referring to specific professionals or organizations can easily influence a professional's judgment. It does not take long for personal interests to begin rivaling client interests. You must avoid kickbacks and fee splitting.

Here is the bottom line: The experience your client has with the professional to whom you refer will be a direct reflection of you and your regard for the client. Be selective in making referrals.

Key Components

- *Refer to other competent professionals when you can no longer be effective.*
- *Take time to explain the reason for the referral.*
- *Know the boundaries of your competence; refer to protect clients' best interests.*
- *Never refer merely for personal gratification or benefit.*

36
Encourage Second Opinions

A seasoned physician specializing in the treatment of cystic fibrosis and other progressive genetic disorders in children, Laura was one of the foremost experts on children's respiratory disorders in the country. Parents often traveled a considerable distance to have their children evaluated and treated in Laura's institute, located within a medical center. Laura sometimes surprised these parents by requesting that they have their children evaluated by other experts in the field—particularly when Laura was recommending a more invasive or experimental approach to care. In light of her stature in the field, parents—and sometimes colleagues—were surprised by the ease and frequency with which Laura encouraged and requested second opinions regarding her diagnoses and treatment recommendations. Rather than feel defensive or reticent about having her work scrutinized by colleagues, Laura welcomed these consultations as an opportunity to verify her conclusions, protect her patients, and, often, learn a thing or two in the process. This openness and patient-first approach ensured unshakable loyalty in parents and profound respect among peers.

If you really care about those you serve, you'll ask them to consult with other professionals at times. Encouraging your clients to get second, third, or fourth opinions from other experts—particularly before making a big decision or embarking on a risky course—is one more way to watch out for their best interests. Avoid becoming defensive when consumers request another professional opinion, and encourage second opinions when you have any doubts about your conclusions and recommendations. Remember this above all else: It's not about you; it's always about the client.

If the thought of referring those you serve to other professionals to get second opinions or check the validity of your work gives you pause, it may be time to do some serious reflecting. If you worry about a colleague seeing your work, reading your reports, or scrutinizing your conclusions and recommendations, there is good reason to ask *why*. What are you trying to hide? Are you operating outside the boundaries of your established competence? Is your work subpar? Are you afraid of professional embarrassment? Is your professional esteem really that fragile? Regardless of what underlies your reticence to encourage second opinions—ego, arrogance, shame, or fear—it is time to get those agendas in check and put your clients' interests first.

Second opinions have saved countless lives in medicine, billions of dollars in business and finance, and untold numbers of wrongful convictions in court. Asking those you serve to get another professional's opinion serves many functions: (1) It helps to confirm that you have not missed something crucial; (2) it offers a check on the quality of your work; (3) it increases the chances that fresh ideas and cutting-edge alternatives will be included in the range of options presented to clients; and (4) it may reassure your clients that your opinions are shared by other experts.

Here is an interesting paradox: The most ethical and client-centered professionals tend to be those with the most acute awareness of their limitations. Healthy professionals recognize their imperfections. They accept their propensity to make errors and have blind spots. Far from denying their own fallibility, they use this knowledge to create safety nets in the form of strong relationships with colleagues willing to offer consultation and advice. Here is the irony: The more humble and self-aware we are, the safer our clients ultimately will be.

Ethical professionals do not merely comply with client requests for referrals and second opinions. They anticipate and initiate these referrals—often long before a client recognizes that this may be helpful. During the informed consent process, these professionals emphasize the potential value of alternative opinions and apprise those they serve that such referrals may be made to ensure that clients get the finest services possible. Ethical professionals often create or join consultation groups made up of other professionals. In these groups, they can get peer supervision of their work. As long as client identities are masked, this is an excellent strategy for arranging routine supervision of work—especially for difficult cases.

But when it comes to referring clients to colleagues for second opinions, be sure to refer only to professionals who will be honest and forthright on all occasions, even if it means they question or refute your conclusions. When your clients' best interests—possibly even their physical or financial health—are on the line, there can be no tolerance for "yes" people or sycophants. Avoid the *Emperor's New Clothes* scenario and refer only to colleagues who'll prioritize clients' best interests the same way you do—colleagues who will tell you when you're naked (or off base professionally). Finally, if you happen to believe that the consulting professional is incorrect, tell your clients and perhaps encourage another consultation; stick to your guns to protect your clients, not your ego.

Key Components

- *Tell clients in advance that you sometimes recommend second opinions.*
- *Routinely seek consultation and supervision from trusted colleagues.*
- *Refer those you serve for second opinions whenever you think such a referral will protect them and help ensure the correct course of action.*
- *Accept your human fallibility, and refuse to get defensive about peer scrutiny.*

37
Resolve Conflicts Flexibly

Shortly after taking command of a fleet hospital in Iraq, Commander Jones, a navy medical service corps officer and health-care administrator, discovered a medical system in disarray. Shortages in medical supplies, inadequate staffing of the hospital, and long delays in transferring critical cases to other facilities threatened to undermine the hospital's mission. When he called his counterpart at the main medical facility—an army hospital—100 miles away, he got an angry earful from the army colonel in charge. The colonel was inexplicably terse, accusing, and disparaging of navy medicine. Less than 24 hours later, Commander Jones startled the colonel by walking into his office, having hopped on the first helicopter flight that morning. The army colonel was even more surprised by Commander Jones's calm, genuine, and flexible demeanor. He listened carefully to the colonel's tirade about the previous navy commander and empathized with his anger. He apologized for his predecessor's unprofessional behavior, asked how he could best support the colonel, and inquired about how the two of them could move ahead to achieve their joint mission—caring for American and Iraqi wounded. Their conversation spilled over to a cordial lunch and was followed up by almost daily phone calls, good-natured bets over the army-navy football game, and growing collegial friendship. Supplies, staffing, and transportation radically improved, as did morale.

Conflict is inevitable. All of us will find ourselves in disagreement with those we serve. When conflict occurs, the ethical question for the professional is, can you prevent a disagreement from becoming a full scale battle? Keeping our sights on clients' best interests, professionals must make diffusing conflict an art form. At times, preventing everyday relationship fender benders from escalating to head-on collisions requires all our resources.

As a human being, we are disadvantaged by an evolved brain that still contains remnants of our primitive past. Some of these remnants predispose us to bypass reason and act out in rage when personal gratification or immediate goal attainment are blocked. When threatened or challenged, we seem programmed to fight. Perhaps this is why anthropologist Margaret Mead proclaimed that the most pressing problem for humankind was how to do away with warfare as a primary method for solving conflicts. Far too many professionals escalate conflicts with clients and colleagues, losing sight of their primary obligation to those they serve. As reward for their anger-fanning behavior, they will hear from attorneys when clients file lawsuits, from licensing boards when clients complain, and from professional organizations when colleagues have had enough.

Here is the good news: As a human being, you also have the antidote to your own conflict-pursuing nature. Reason, empathy, and commitment to ethical ideals can serve to diffuse destructive emotions and refocus your attention on those you serve. Professionals are obligated to combat aggressive impulses and strive only to benefit those they serve while avoiding any harm. When inevitable conflicts occur, professionals must resolve them responsibly with the least possible harm to clients.

Conflict resolution is an ethical imperative and should be a foundational skill set for all professionals. Resolving conflict is a process—not an event—aimed at reducing polarization. Good conflict resolution often incorporates conciliation, negotiation, or, when some ongoing disagreement is inevitable, a civil decision to agree to disagree.

If there are salient ingredients to conflict resolution, they must certainly include the interpersonal skill of *active listening*, the moral virtue of *caring*, and the cognitive capacity for *flexibility*. Deliberate and open-minded listening may do more to diffuse conflict than any other professional skill. Taking time to thoroughly listen to a client's or colleague's perspective may reveal a simple misunderstanding or may shed light on a perspective previously ignored. Listening communicates empathy and positive regard. It is hard to be angry with someone who is actively trying to hear another's perspective. Often, listening is closely linked to the larger moral commitment of caring. A professional who has internalized the virtue of caring is more acutely attuned to the best interests of others and less dogmatically driven toward self-promotion. Finally, in all things, be flexible. Conflict is synonymous with polarization. Cataclysmic wars occur when both sides dig in, refusing to budge or even dialogue with the opposing side. Ineffective professionals are rigid, dogmatic, and entrenched in rule and procedure. They lose sight of the reason most rules and procedures exist—to protect and serve others.

One of your most challenging professional obligations may be to address unethical or inappropriate behavior in colleagues and peers. All of us are obligated to confront colleagues who may be threatening the best interests of clients, the public at large, or our profession. It is not a question of *should* you confront a colleague, but *how*. Here is a guarantee: Turning a collegial confrontation into a personal attack or an accusation-laced tirade will always backfire. The most effective professionals among us approach bad-behaving colleagues with evident compassion and concern. They show respect and empathy to elicit cooperation, and they always refrain from making unfounded accusations or pejorative comments.

Kindness, caring, deliberate listening, and abiding flexibility will work miracles when it comes to preventing and diffusing conflict.

Key Components

- *Be flexible in all interactions and negotiations with others.*
- *Prevent conflict through clear communication.*
- *Listen carefully and express empathy as a means of depolarizing relationships.*
- *Remember that professionals place the interests of clients first.*

5

Exercising Caution

Matters of Prudence

Prudent professionals not only *know* what is right but also *do* what is right. They nurture a sense of wisdom born of experience. They employ forethought, deliberate weighing of options, sound judgment, and discretion in all of their professional activities. In their practical day-to-day affairs and in all interactions with people, prudent professionals demonstrate clear-sightedness and thoroughness.

In this chapter, we focus on the components of ethical practice most directly related to the moral virtue of prudence. Prudent professionals think carefully before acting, recognizing the danger inherent in impulsive decision making. They prevent conflicts of interest by avoiding mixed roles, honoring the boundaries between their professional and personal lives, and remaining attuned to their own agendas. Prudent professionals are averse to overstating facts and making unsupported and grandiose claims. They are given to thoughtful and thorough documentation of their work, and they understand that great care in describing their assessments, interventions, and recommendations is always in their clients' best interests. Prudence demands that professionals delegate assignments only to those who have appropriate training and supervision. They exercise particular caution when presented with gifts and favors. In responding to gifts, they consider clients' best interests, potential conflicts, and the motivation behind the giving. Finally, prudent professionals only promise what they can actually deliver, and they make good on the delivery.

38
Evaluate before Acting

Over the course of a 25-year career, Shandra had earned the respect of her elementary education colleagues. As a school psychologist, Shandra's job was to conduct psychological testing of children in the district with very complicated problems including learning disorders, attention difficulties, autism, and various mood problems. It was common for distraught parents, frustrated teachers, and school administrators to try to push her for rapid diagnoses and instantaneous changes to children's educational plans. But Shandra was famous for putting the breaks on these demands. She had learned the hard way. Rushing an assessment just to meet someone's demand increased the likelihood of a misdiagnosis and subsequent harm to a child who invariably would receive an inappropriate intervention. Before rendering a diagnosis and recommending remediation, Shandra carefully reviewed all available records, performing a full battery of psychological tests, conducted behavior observations of the child in the classroom; interviewed parents and teachers as well as the child; and, when necessary, consulted with colleagues to get a second opinion. Her prudent and thorough approach resulted in uncanny diagnostic accuracy, generations of positively impacted children, and a well-deserved reputation for professional excellence.

Rushing to judgment is easy. Wrought with pitfalls, however, rushing to judgment can have horrendous consequences. Do not take action without careful assessment. Imagine a surgeon scrubbing for the ER without ordering lab tests, an accountant offering financial planning without reviewing records, or a lawyer heading to trial without having a solid grasp of the evidence. Professionalism is synonymous with planning. The ethical professional thinks, gathers relevant data, and carefully considers the best options for clients before embarking on a course of action.

Professional ethics codes require that professionals demonstrate prudence, forethought, and informed calculation on behalf of the people they serve. Prudent professionals make good decisions, largely because they are willing to defer action until they have adequately evaluated all relevant facts. Professionals base opinions and recommendations on information and assessment techniques sufficient to substantiate their findings.

If prudence has an enemy, its name is *impulse*. In the culture of the "now," where instant gratification is the norm, clients and colleagues may push for immediate action and demand immediate results. But impulsive professionals don't last long. Hotheaded decisions and undue haste lead quickly to error, embarrassment, and regret. Yet impulsivity is part of the human condition. Consider the infamous marshmallow experiment conducted at Stanford University (Goleman, 1995; Shoda, Mischel, & Peake, 1990). Four-year-olds were left alone in a room with a marshmallow and promised another one only if they could wait 20 minutes before eating the first. Those who were able to wait turned out to be better adjusted and more dependable adolescents many years later. They also scored nearly 200 points better on the SATs than those who could not wait, and they were less likely to use drugs or experience teen pregnancy. Later in life as professionals, the people who earlier in life gratify emotional impulse and act without forethought are more likely to commit malpractice—often harming others and embarrassing the profession in the process.

By modeling delayed gratification and thoughtful consideration, ethical professionals may help those they serve to overcome their own impulsivity. They are exemplars of self-restraint. In much the same way, marriage counselors teach troubled couples to evaluate before acting. When conflict arises or a critical decision about the relationship must be made, it's advisable to slow down the process, buy time, think carefully, and eschew haste. In essence, look before leaping.

Keep in mind that thoughtful evaluation need not be incompatible with creativity or intuition. Seasoned professionals discover the right balance between cold analysis and intuitive insight in their work. They may move quickly when the evidence warrants such action, but they are suspicious of "hunches" and loath to act without a clear view of the road ahead.

To avoid regret as a professional, base your work on sound assessment procedures and processes. Take the time required to gather and analyze salient data, and base your work on valid evidence.

Key Components

- *Refuse to act on impulse or emotion.*
- *Carefully assess and evaluate relevant variables before taking action.*
- *Consider the consequences of all available courses of action.*
- *Model self-restraint and delayed gratification in your work.*

39
Avoid Conflicts of Interest

Andrew was the governor-appointed zoning commissioner for a midsize Southwest city. With property values rising and more companies interested in establishing operations in the area, Andrew and his zoning commission felt increasing pressure from business leaders and politicians to create more business-friendly zoning. Given their considerable workload during the previous year, Andrew decided to arrange a three-day retreat for his personnel. He allowed his office staff to take care of all retreat planning. He was shocked when it was announced that the retreat would be held at a very pricey waterfront resort and inquired about how this could possibly fit within his modest retreat budget. He learned that an international automobile manufacturer—one with strong interest in building a plant near the city—had contacted his staff and offered to fund all retreat accommodations. Andrew immediately contacted the company, thanked it sincerely for the offer, and declined to accept any financial assistance for the retreat. Rather than chastise his staff, he looked at himself and recognized his own oversight, not adequately training his staff. He then called an impromptu meeting, using this experience as a teachable moment, and explained the ethical problems inherent in conflicts of interest. He increased the retreat budget to allow for very comfortable—if not luxurious—accommodations and was certain to include an ethics workshop on the upcoming training schedule.

Human beings are self-interested. As humans, professionals occasionally develop interests that clash with those of their clients, customers, vendors, or other people vying for a benefit. Yet professionals must put aside personal interests when they conflict with the best interests of those they serve.

Avoiding conflicts of interest is a fundamental ethical imperative. A conflict of interest may occur any time we take on a professional role in which personal, professional, legal, financial, or other interests may either impair our effectiveness or cause harm or exploitation to those we serve. When motivated by financial reward, professional advantage, or even romantic interest, we easily lose objectivity and behave ineffectively in our professional role. Too many professionals learn their lessons too late. Not until they are under scrutiny of an ethics panel or court of law do they come to terms with their conflict of interests and the damage it causes.

Be aware that certain professional contexts heighten the risk of conflicted interests. For instance, when working for an organization and simultaneously serving individual clients, a professional may discover that the best interests of the organization (e.g., a health insurer, an investment company, the government) may conflict with the interests of an individual served by the organization (e.g., a medical patient, an investor, an employee). In this case, the professional may allow direct or implied threats from the organization to color professional decisions vis-à-vis the individual.

Keep in mind that conflicts of interest need not produce clear evidence of harm or exploitation. Just the perception that you are serving your own interests can damage your reputation or the public image of your profession. The perception that you are benefiting inappropriately from a professional relationship can cast doubt on your integrity and judgment. Ethical professionals respect their human vulnerability, the temptation of personal interests, and the need to erect and honor iron-clad prohibitions around entering potentially exploitive relationships.

If there is any significant danger of conflict between your personal interests and those of the people you serve, avoid entering the relationship in the first place. If a conflict of interest emerges in the context of your professional work, attempt to make a suitable referral or work with your client to resolve the conflict with an emphasis on his or her best interest.

Key Components

- *Respect your own vulnerability to self-interest.*
- *Avoid relationships that have great potential for a conflict of interest.*
- *Refuse simultaneous professional and nonprofessional roles with those you serve.*
- *Recognize that even the perception of a conflict of interest can cast doubts on your integrity and judgment.*
- *When conflicts of interest arise, stop the conflict and make good use of referrals.*

40
Set and Honor Boundaries

In some respects, Marcus took a novel approach to his work as a successful divorce attorney. He encouraged mediation and counseling as an avenue to prevent divorce, and, when unavoidable, to reduce the hostility and self-defeating bickering that characterized many divorcing couples. Marcus's calm, reasonable, and reassuring demeanor made him both effective and "therapeutic" in his work. He discovered early in his career that clients often were overwrought, emotionally needy, and vulnerable when they were dissolving their marriages. In the beginning, he became overly invested emotionally in his clients and once or twice found himself on the verge of allowing a romantic relationship to evolve. He was grateful when a reliable mentor reminded him of his ethical responsibility to place his clients' interests first and to avoid blurring professional boundaries in his work. Over the years, he fine-tuned the delicate balance between offering emo-

tional support and encouragement to distressed, lonely clients while main-
taining clear boundaries—boundaries that strictly prohibited close friend-
ships, romantic connections, business partnerships, or other nonprofessional
relationships. Marcus accepted solid boundaries as one of the requirements
of professionalism and was quick to consult with a trusted colleague when-
ever he felt the urge to cross the line.

Cancer is a horrific group of diseases, responsible for about 13 percent of all deaths. Three salient properties differentiate cancerous tumors from benign ones: (1) Cancerous tumors are *aggressive* in that they grow and divide limitlessly; (2) they are *invasive* in that they cross over into and destroy surrounding tissue; and (3) they are *metastatic* in that they spread to other regions of the body. Collectively, these characteristics of cancerous tumors compromise the human body's healthy functioning.

Boundaries are an inherent characteristic of healthy systems. All systems consist of component parts, and in order for these parts to retain their identity and function properly, they must maintain their boundaries. As boundaries break down, component parts lose their identity and fail to function properly; left unchecked, the system malfunctions.

Strong boundaries are basic to healthy professional relationships. Boundaries are the buffers or barriers between a professional and a client, preventing the relationship from becoming something other than professional, reducing the chances the relationship will be compromised, and minimizing the possibility of negative outcomes for clients. Wise professionals self-impose moratoriums on avoidable extraprofessional (e.g., social, business, romantic) exchanges with those they serve. Professionals who kindly but firmly establish and then honor limits on nonprofessional contact are less likely to violate the trust of clients or cause them unintended harm.

Boundaries in professional relationships are important for several reasons. First, clients assume that professionals will focus the full force of their expertise on clients' needs. As professionals manipulate their relationships and the priority shifts to the gratification of their personal needs, the risk for misunderstanding and unintended harm increases. Second, professional relationships always involve a power differential. The wholesale trust and dependency characteristic of some clients makes another kind of relationship (e.g., sexual) outside the realm of acceptability. Third, clients often come to professionals for the express purpose of finding a safe place in which to openly share their feelings and become vulnerable. Such vulnerability can heighten the risk of exploitation. Fourth, when professionals blur boundaries with clients, they simultaneously lose objectivity and undermine their own effectiveness. Undue familiarity and multiple roles with clients heighten the risk of conflicts of interest, exploitation, and poor service delivery.

Although strong boundaries are a cornerstone of ethical practice, rigidity can be problematic. When professionals become excessively zealous—even preoccupied—with ironclad professional fences, clients may perceive them as dogmatic, inflexible, and more concerned about self-protection (risk management) than their welfare as clients. Concern for boundaries is no excuse to become sterile, stoic, and cold. The most effective professionals recognize that boundaries exist for clients, not themselves. They also recognize that at times, certain benign *boundary crossings* (e.g., accepting a small gift from a client, occasionally extending the length of a session, meeting in the home of an ill client, touching a client on the shoulder or arm for support, offering a supportive self-disclosure related to the client's experience) may be quite helpful. Such flexibility communicates your humanness and emotional texture. It can deepen clients' trust and sense of safety without compromising more important boundaries.

How can a professional effectively establish and respectfully honor boundaries and yet allow appropriate boundary crossings while avoiding *boundary violations*? Think of boundary violations as intrusions into the client's physical or psychological space. Like cancer's invasion of adjacent cells, boundary violations are uninvited, likely to cause harm, and inconsistent with the professional's primary obligations to the client. Boundary violations also have the potential for metastasizing and causing damage beyond the professional relationship. It is evident that the ethical professional must strike a delicate balance between honoring boundaries and remaining sensitive to the needs of specific clients in specific circumstances. This could not be more important than in working with clients from other cultures. Culturally based differences involving appropriate personal space, use of touch, self-disclosure, and gift giving must be considered when navigating boundaries.

When considering crossing boundaries with a client, here are several key recommendations: (1) Be sure you are motivated by the client's needs, not your own; (2) ask yourself whether the crossing is necessary to facilitate your work for the client; (3) discuss the boundary crossing up front to reduce misunderstanding; (4) consider how the boundary crossing might, or might not, fit with the client's background and culture; (5) consider the power differential in the relationship and the risk of harm; and (6) consult with a respected colleague when the issues are muddy.

When it comes to decisions about professional boundaries, always remember your primary charge vis-à-vis clients: to be a *virtuous agent*. A virtuous agent asks, "Who shall I be?" when considering a boundary crossing or blurred roles with clients. The ethical professional employs wisdom, self-awareness, caution, sensitivity to culture, and an unflagging commitment to protecting clients when setting and honoring professional boundaries.

Key Components

- *Set and maintain clear boundaries between your professional and personal life.*
- *Be cautious about blurring roles or crossing boundaries with clients.*
- *Recognize that boundaries protect clients from exploitation and harm.*
- *Appreciate the distinction between boundary crossings and boundary violations.*
- *Consider cultural variables when navigating boundaries.*
- *Seek consultation when contemplating any significant boundary crossing.*

41
Do Not Make Exaggerated Claims

When Janice was assigned as the new manager and head realtor of one of the region's largest realty agencies, times were hard. A two-year decline in home sales and property values had taken the wind out of the market and sharply reduced income for most realtors. The first sign that something was terribly wrong at the agency emerged when the secretary presented Janice with five customer complaints during her first morning on the job. In each case, the customer felt duped or misled by something a realtor said or information the agency had published about a property. Alarmed by these allegations, Janice proceeded to investigate the veracity of each complaint. She also began to visit randomly selected properties listed with the agency and carefully compare the printed ad with the properties themselves. She went even further and called several customers whose property purchases were pending and asked about promises and claims made by her realtors. The results of her investigation were distressing. Across the agency, there was a clear pattern of publishing misleading information about properties; making inaccurate claims about crime rates, school quality, and resale values; and even making erroneous guarantees. Janice immediately fired the worst offenders, disciplined others, and established clear guidelines bearing on truth in advertising. She also worked to resolve each complaint in a manner satisfactory to the misled customers.

Federal trade laws mandate truth in advertising. These laws make it illegal for businesses to make false claims about their products, goods, or services. Their advertising must be truthful and non-deceptive, make claims that are backed up by evidence, and be presented fairly. The purpose of these laws is to prevent predatory practices that benefit businesses and injure "reasonable consumers"—typical individuals who look at ads and place their faith in the veracity of businesses' claims.

Where did truth in advertising come from? It grew out of a context in which dishonesty ran rampant in corporate America. Just as dishonesty in advertising is illegal, making misleading or exaggerated claims in your professional work is wrong. When you embellish or inflate the benefits of your services or products such that your claims are fraudulent, inaccurate, or unsupported by evidence, you have failed to demonstrate prudence and integrity.

It seems that *puffery*—the tendency to exaggerate or magnify beyond the limits of truth—is part of the human condition. But specific factors exacerbate the tendency toward puffery. Exaggeration and misrepresentation are more common among professionals who (1) are too pressed for time to gather evidence regarding the outcomes of their services; (2) practice unusual or "fringe" techniques for which little scientific evidence exists; (3) distance themselves from colleagues and fail to seek routine consultation or remain up-to-date with regard to current research and best practices in their specialty; (4) fail to carefully review the work of others who advertise or promote their professional services; (5) are under significant financial pressure; or (6) are prone to cutting corners and exaggerating as a general character trait.

Whatever the temptation to exaggerate claims about your products or services, remember this: Professionals are compelled by ethical standards to base their opinions, claims, and recommendations on established knowledge in their field—preferably knowledge rooted in thoughtful scientific research or careful accumulation of documented cases and professional experience. Therefore, ethical professionals are scrupulous about preparing and reviewing brochures, advertisements, online information, and all other descriptions of their services. They understand that they are the ones ultimately responsible for the accuracy of information promulgated by advertising and promotional agencies.

Although very few professionals would fabricate evidence to bolster claims about their services—an egregious ethical violation in any profession—some may be tempted to cut corners when rendering assessments and recommendations. Ethical professionals base their opinions, conclusions, and evaluations on information and techniques suitable to substantiate their findings. Professionals must remain sensitive to the fact that their assessment results often have significant consequences for those assessed.

Here is the bottom line: Only make claims and render opinions that can clearly be supported by appropriate evidence. If in doubt about the legitimacy of a professional ad or product claim, ask your-self, "What would a jury of my peers have to say after reading this?" If you were questioned, would you have adequate evidence to support your claim?

Key Components

- *Never make unsupportable or grandiose claims about your products or services.*
- *Remember that overstating facts may harm consumers and clients.*
- *Base all professional opinions, statements, and recommendations on information and evidence sufficient to substantiate them.*
- *Always screen promotional work done by employees or other agencies.*

42
Document Carefully

A general practice physician in rural Alaska, Frank spent much of his time piloting a single-engine plane to remote villages where medical services were badly needed. He saw most of his patients once a year at best, and much of his work involved triage at the scene of accidents or the provision of emergency care until a patient could be airlifted hundreds of miles to a hospital. When the weather was rough, he often was limited to providing radio consultation to a nurse or a medical technician. He or she would pro-vide direct patient care until Frank could arrive. Frank discovered early the importance of detailed documentation. The documentation helped ensure that his patients were well cared for when they were transported for emer-gency care. Receiving physicians and remote medical service providers re-lied on Frank's careful assessments and clear treatment plans. His work enabled them to provide rapid interventions and avoid the loss of precious time repeating exams. His colleagues came to respect and appreciate his thorough documentation in patient medical records. His attention to detail saved more than one life. When pressed about why he took such care to keep all his patient records up-to-date, Frank would also admit that piloting a plane in rural Alaska could be dangerous. In the event of his own incapac-

ity or death, he was committed to ensuring that his successor could step in without missing a beat.

Documents serve an important function in society. They communicate information, often of an official or legal nature. According to professor John Searle (1995), documents help construct social reality: They represent a person or group's thinking, intentions, and obligations. Theoretically, documents are immutable, indicating that the thinking, intention, and obligation contained in them remain in perpetuity unless a specific time frame is designated in them. To *document* (verb) means to create a *document* (noun), which is accomplished by collecting, organizing, distilling, and crafting information relative to one's professional purposes.

While documentation often is necessary, careful documentation is paramount. Slipshod documentation and record keeping suggests incompetence, inattention to details, or inadequate delivery of professional services. Clear documentation can enhance the quality of your work. It also may save you considerable grief should things go awry in a professional relationship. Psychologist Ed Nottingham says that documentation can be a "best ally," just as the absence of documentation—or the wrong kind of documentation—can be devastating (Smith, 2003).

The primary goal of careful documentation is to better serve your customers. Secondarily, solid records help prevent misunderstandings or accusations of substandard work. Excellent attention to detail in the documentation of your work helps achieve the following objectives:

- Ensuring that your work is high-quality and carefully tailored to the problem or request the client presents.
- Creating a record of your assessment and development of an appropriate plan for intervention or care.
- Detailing dates of service, specific services delivered, fees, and contractual arrangements.
- Affording an opportunity to reflect on the customer's progress and the efficacy of the services offered.

- Providing enough detail about your services such that another professional could continue services should termination or transfer become necessary.
- Offering clear evidence of your professional plan, decision making, communications with the customer, and consultations received should your work ever be challenged in a lawsuit or ethics complaint.

Although records must be created primarily to better serve your customers, they also provide essential insurance against wrongful complaints or charges of malpractice. Professional relationships occasionally turn out badly—at times because clients are unreasonable or prone to conflict. A carefully constructed and updated record helps your peers (on ethics panels) and the legal system (in the case of a lawsuit) observe your rationale and implementation of a plan over the course of the relationship. The record also should document your efforts at diffusing conflict and collaborating with customers when problems arise. Professionals working in high-risk settings or with conflict-prone customers should be especially vigilant to thorough documentation. When documenting your professional work, imagine that a jury of your peers is looking over your shoulder at the quality, professionalism, and detail of your work.

Finally, don't forget to assiduously protect customer records. All records should be considered confidential and protected accordingly. Ensure that your staff is well trained in this regard. Abide by state and federal guidelines relevant to the storage, maintenance, and disposal of records. In many instances, records must be maintained for a minimum number of years. In other instances, records are best maintained in perpetuity. Again, careful documentation of your work better serves your customers. Take this facet of practice just as seriously as your personal interactions with clients.

Key Components

- *Carefully document your professional work as a means of better serving your customers and ensuring an accurate record.*

- *Create a record of your assessments, decision making, and efforts to track the outcomes of your work.*
- *Abide by relevant legal statutes and professional ethical standards bearing on professional records.*
- *Thoroughly document efforts to diffuse conflict, seek consultation, and serve the best interests of angry or accusing customers.*
- *Protect customer confidentiality in the maintenance and disposal of records.*

43
Delegate Thoughtfully, Monitor Closely

After 20 years in the forensic arena, Raphael clearly understood the value and the liability associated with supervising interns. A licensed social worker with considerable expertise in child custody evaluations, Raphael often supervised two or three social-work interns from an excellent local university graduate program. He was very careful to thoroughly train his interns in the art of interviewing witnesses, reviewing records, and objectively observing parent-child interactions. He was equally careful to ensure that interns understood activities in which they could not engage (e.g., interviewing parents and children, administering tests, speaking with attorneys). He carefully reviewed each intern's work on practice cases before ever allowing the intern to participate in an actual case. Raphael always informed both his clients and the courts that interns would assist in very limited ways with the evaluation, but he emphasized that he supervised each intern and ultimately was responsible for all aspects of each evaluation. Raphael's prudent approach to delegating work resulted in a more efficient evaluation process without compromising the quality of the reports rendered to the court.

Successful professionals who advance in their careers typically get promoted to higher-level positions. As professionals assume greater responsibility, their taking on administrative or supervisory roles is inevitable. And taking on these roles means delegating responsibility. But some professionals may be competent in their fields yet incompetent as supervisors. Here is the question: How can you delegate to subordinates without compromising the quality of your services to consumers? Thoughtful delegation is an essential component of ethical practice.

Chances are you'll work with some combination of supervisees, junior associates, assistants, students, and numerous office staff during your career. You may work with a variety of these subordinates at one time. As a supervisor, you have the essential role of empowering your subordinates to serve as your representative and carry out various tasks associated with your professional work. Excellent mentors, supervisors, and managers learn that wise delegation is a hallmark of effective mentoring. Here is the criteria they should use in delegating tasks: (1) Subordinates should have the adequate education, training, and experience required to perform their duties competently; (2) subordinates should not have any conflict of interest or preexisting relationship with the client they will serve; and (3) subordinates should be carefully supervised and monitored, providing the guarantee that the services are performed competently.

Professionals who get into trouble in this area may rely too much on subordinates or trainees, fail to assess their actual competence, provide inadequate supervision of their work, or be experiencing financial stress or strain compelling them to increase output and income by overtaxing them. Whatever your motivation, remember this: You *always* hold ultimate responsibility for the services rendered by those under your supervision. Before allowing individuals to serve as your emissaries or assistants, make sure that they thoroughly understand the limits of their scope of practice. Clearly define roles, establish routine supervision, and carefully evaluate subordinates' competence. Also, if specific techniques require specialized training (e.g., psychological tests, laboratory analyses, legal briefs, financial estimates), be certain your subordinates have the requisite skills and supervised experience *before* allowing them to work with customers.

Many jurisdictions make it a crime to aid another person in the practice of a profession when the person is not credentialed or licensed as a professional. To protect the public, it is essential to restrict the delegation of specific tasks related to your professional work to those with appropriate training and supervision. Never allow a subordinate to falsely convey credentials to customers. Consult state guidelines and professional standards to determine which tasks may be delegated to competent assistants.

Key Components

- *Before delegating any task, make sure that your subordinate is competent.*
- *Consult state and professional guidelines to determine which tasks are appropriate to delegate to nonprofessionals.*
- *Closely monitor and supervise the work of those to whom you delegate tasks.*
- *Make sure that your subordinates do not have conflicts of interest or multiple relationships with the customers they serve.*

44
Think Twice about Accepting Gifts

A successful financial planner, Lars had a reputation for taking on several pro bono cases each month—typically involving low-income adults who'd gotten into serious financial trouble. Although unlikely to generate much revenue from these clients, Lars was thorough and patient in assessing each client's situation, carefully teaching the money management basics, and providing enough encouragement and oversight to get them back on track. Because his impact on the lives of these lower-income clients was dramatic, it was not atypical for a client to present him with a gift over the holidays or as the relationship drew to a close. On these occasions, Lars was quick to evaluate several important factors such as the monetary value of the gift, the client's apparent motivation for giving it, any hidden agendas likely associated with the gift, and what gift giving might mean for the client—particularly in light of his or her cultural background. While keeping his clients' best interests in mind, and remaining conscious of the danger of exploitation, Lars generally accepted thank-you cards, very inexpensive trinkets, or baked goods, but he politely declined anything more expensive. He explained that accepting

gifts beyond his professional fee was prohibited by his professional code
and that his clients' heartfelt thanks offered ample reward.

As the ancient Greeks discovered on accepting the Trojan horse, gifts have the potential to wreak havoc. In professional life, gifts come in many forms such as small keepsakes, free services, entertainment, or food items. Clients also have been known to offer extravagant furnishings, cars, or cash. Gifts may be a genuine expression of innocent gratitude or a malignant attempt to manipulate. It is the professional's duty to be cautious regarding gifts and to keep the focus on the client's best interest.

Although accepting certain gifts under certain circumstances may be both ethically defensible and helpful to clients, we begin with the premise that professionals should not accept gifts from clients. Here are some reasons why. First, professionals' primary obligation is to maintain thorough commitment and fidelity to their clients. If you are profiting from your relationship with a client—beyond the appropriate and contracted reimbursement for your services—something is wrong. Clients are often in the power-down position. They are vulnerable. Profiting from a client's propensity to give gifts may blind you to the possibility of exploitation. Second, client motivations for gift giving are difficult to decipher and their motivations may change over time. Why is this client giving this specific gift at this point in the professional relationship and in this unique context? What does the gift symbolize to your client? Seemingly innocuous gift cards or symbolic knick-knacks may hold powerful meaning for the giver. For instance, is the gift intended to curry special favor? Is the client working hard to please you? Is the client making a desperate effort to maintain the relationship? Could the gift be a subtle romantic invitation? Even when a gift is given with benign motivation, remember that the giver's perception of the experience may shift with time. Professionals have run afoul of ethics committees after accepting an extravagant gift from a client (e.g., family heirlooms, jewelry, artwork) only to have the client—or his or her family members—later report feeling exploited.

A third reason to avoid accepting gifts is the simple fact that appearances matter. Even when a gift is inexpensive, given with benign motivations, and in no way intended to influence your work, remember that your peers, the public, and the client's family members may see things quite differently. Others may reasonably infer that you are accepting gifts that may either exploit clients or be designed to influence your professional decisions. It always is inappropriate to directly or indirectly solicit a gift from a client. Furthermore, it is inappropriate to take advantage of a client's vulnerability or to accept a gift that may create a conflict of interest or cloud professional judgment.

Should professionals refuse all gifts all the time? Such a policy—particularly if clearly communicated to clients at the outset of every relationship—would prevent gifts from undermining your fiduciary responsibilities. But refusing all gifts may actually diminish your effectiveness and reduce the quality of your interpersonal connections to some of the people you serve. On some occasions, cards, baked goods, or very small tokens of appreciation may be deeply meaningful as expressions of gratitude. Refusing to accept such gifts may be perceived as a rejection or insult by members of certain cultures. Gracefully accepting these tokens may bolster your efficacy, cement a solid working relationship, and allow a client the pleasure of expressing gratitude.

Think carefully before accepting a client's gift. Look for red flags such as extravagant items, inappropriate connotations associated with the gift, the appearance of impropriety, the potential for exploitation, misguided motivations, or recurrent gift giving. In all cases, ask yourself: Is this really in my client's best interest? Finally, watch out for self-justifying. If you believe you really *deserve* a gift, your motives no doubt are misguided.

Key Components

- *Remember that faithfulness to your client's best interests usually prohibits the possibility of profiting from the relationship by accepting gifts.*

- *Carefully consider a client's motivations for giving a gift before accepting it.*
- *Be sensitive to the potential for exploitation and the appearance of impropriety.*
- *Communicate up front any policy proscribing gifts.*
- *Remain sensitive to the meaning of gift giving from the client's cultural perspective.*
- *Check your underlying motivation if you believe you deserve a gift from a client.*

45
Make Conservative Estimates

Linden was a respected endocrine system researcher at the National Institutes of Health. Thyroid gland functioning was her specialty. Beloved by journal editors and funding sources, Linden had a sterling reputation for timely delivery of her end-of-year grant reports, and when invited to contribute an article to a journal, she always delivered on time. Her secret was a cautious and thoughtful approach to estimating delivery dates. Understanding that life was often "crazy" and unpredictable, she always multiplied her initial estimates by three so as to build in plenty of buffer space for the rabbit trails and dead ends so common in medical research. When one of Linden's animal studies suggested the possibility of a radical breakthrough in the treatment of damaged glands, she received considerable pressure from her supervisor and from the media to suggest that the discovery would entirely shift the medical profession's approach to treating human endocrine problems. But Linden understood the difference between animal and human models, and the need for replication and extension of the research to other animals before applying the science to humans. Although her reserved approach frustrated some, her prudence was rewarded when subsequent research showed little effect in people with endocrine disorders.

Prudence demands the exercise of good judgment, forethought, and appropriate caution. Thoughtful professionals recognize the danger of making promises they cannot reasonably expect to fulfill. They opt for conservative estimates when contracting for services, taking into account the probability of unexpected delays, hassles, and negative outcomes. Conservative estimates protect clients from harm caused by erroneous expectations and unfulfilled promises.

Protecting clients from harm and avoiding misleading statements demand that professionals assume caution when estimating the benefits and reasonable time frame for their services. Because our estimates, predictions, and promises can have dramatic effects on those we serve, we must be cautious when predicting what students will learn in an educational program, what a surgical procedure will yield, what verdict a defendant can anticipate, what return might be expected on an investment, and on what date a manuscript can be delivered.

Whatever you are asked to estimate or predict, use a conservative approach and carefully consider the support for your estimates. Would a committee of your peers come to a similar conclusion based on the evidence available? When reporting the results of your work, exercise caution in interpreting the findings. Refuse to go beyond the evidence merely for the sake of self-promotion. When estimating when a renovation will be completed or a book manuscript delivered, build in extra time for unexpected surprises and the simple exigencies of daily life. Delivering ahead of schedule always is better. Professionals with a reputation for cautious calculation, scrupulous planning, and impeccable reliability will be positively regarded and generally rewarded with more professional opportunities. Of course, successful professionals must be selective in the work they accept so as to remain punctual and dependable.

Be conservative in your statements and estimates. Make careful predictions bearing on the time frame and the likely outcomes of your work. To do anything else is imprudent and sometimes unethical. And don't forget, erroneous estimates and unfulfilled promises may have legal ramifications, namely fraud and breach of contract.

Key Components

- *Exercise caution when making promises or claims regarding your work.*

- *Be conservative when estimating outcomes or delivery dates.*
- *Don't make matters worse for clients by creating erroneous expectations.*
- *Refuse to inflate, embellish, or misrepresent your work; seek to be honest and accurate in your predictions.*

6

Caring for Others

Matters of Compassion

Arthur Schopenhauer, a nineteenth-century philosopher, claimed that compassion is the basis for all morality. In the classic parable of the Good Samaritan, the passerby answered an internal moral call both to pay attention and to respond to a fellow human being in need. Ethical professionals empathize with people who are stricken by misfortune or suffering. They cannot sit on the sidelines as passive observers, ignoring the plight of individuals whose circumstances are dire. Instead of passivity, they find avenues within the framework of their professional roles to demonstrate compassion in attitude and action.

In this chapter, we hone in on the essential ingredients of care. Key elements include showing positive regard, offering pro bono service, attending to more than the bottom line, and protecting vulnerable people. Compassionate professionals adopt a nonjudgmental attitude and accept people unconditionally, create relationships defined by grace and tolerance, and volunteer some of their professional time and work to those who might otherwise go without services. They remain focused on the interests of specific individuals when applying rules and standards, and show sensitivity to the needs and suffering of vulnerable members of the population.

Compassion stands in opposition to indifference—a dulled, insensitive, and uncaring disposition toward people. To bolster compassion and overcome indifference, professionals must make the habits of care a priority. As professionals' respect for persons develops into care, and as care deepens, amazing human dynamics are set in motion, transforming the landscape of professionalism.

46
Show Positive Regard

A longtime junior high school teacher, Hayes was respected and beloved by his students for both his excellent teaching and his kind, caring disposition. Compassion seemed to come naturally to him. He took a personal interest in his students, went out of his way to help them when they faced difficult circumstances, verbally encouraged them on a regular basis, and generally showed each one appreciation and acceptance. In one instance, he caught Jeremy, a student he was mentoring, cheating on a midterm examination. Hayes reluctantly reported Jeremy to the principal. The principal promptly arranged a conference with Jeremy, his parents, and Hayes. During the meeting, Jeremy made little eye contact. His embarrassment was obvious to everyone present. The principal presented the facts and chastised Jeremy for his indiscreet behavior. Hayes took a different approach. He proceeded to describe all the attributes he most admired in Jeremy and expressed a firm belief that the cheating incident was neither characteristic of Jeremy nor reflective on his future behavior. He offered a compelling case for a modest punishment followed by remediation. Hayes offered to be Jeremy's primary sponsor in this process and expressed genuine positive regard for Jeremy and his potential. Grateful and bolstered by his teacher's faith, Jeremy rose to the occasion and became an exemplar of character as well as a reliable leader among his classmates.

The Dalai Lama has said that if you want others to be happy, practice compassion, and that if you want to be happy, practice compassion. Compassion for others is critical to the character of ethical professionals. Real compassion evidences itself in a deep concern for the welfare of others, a compelling obligation to enhance their well-being, and attempts to reduce their suffering. Compassion, otherwise known as the virtue of care, requires that we set aside personal gain, entrenched attitudes, and sometimes rigid and arbitrary "rules." The purpose of these actions is to prize, protect, and assist those we serve. Ethical professionals must assert in word and deed what philosopher Immanuel Kant described as each person's singular duty as a caring neighbor: *to promote, according to his or her means, the happiness of others who are in need.*

Caring starts with respect. To respect another is to offer *unconditional positive regard*—a favorite phrase coined by master psychotherapist Carl Rogers. Unconditional positive regard takes form in these behaviors:

- Viewing each person as someone of worth, someone with intrinsic value.
- Prizing individuals' unique strengths and recognizing their potential.
- Suspending judgment: never approaching people with an attitude of prejudice, depreciation, or self-serving criticism.
- Accepting people—knowing they have imperfections, make errors, and are fallible—even if you disagree with their choices and opinions.
- Listening carefully to each person so you can understand and communicate understanding.
- Offering warmth in the form of genuine interest and sincere concern.

When professionals acquire a heartfelt respect for other people, such as in the case of a therapist and client, it is possible to treat the client as worthy of assistance even if the client does not appear to *deserve* compassion. As professionals suspend judgment, refuse to assign pejorative labels, and show genuine respect, their caring naturally will flow through their behavior. Their attunement and responsiveness to human needs becomes more apparent.

Along with unconditional positive regard comes an abiding awareness that compassion at times may trump regulations and rules. The virtue of care and its expression in loving concern presents an ethical obligation to enhance the well-being and alleviate the suffering of others. On occasion, this may require professionals to judiciously flex or reconcile laws, regulations, and standards that seem to create irreconcilable conflicts or place a person in a harmful situation. Finally, respect and unconditional positive regard demand that professionals work hard at delivering grace and compassion when a client fails or commits a wrong in the professional relationship. Certainly, wrongdoing should not be overlooked or easily dismissed. And certainly, some wrongdoings carry heavier penalties than others. However, through the lens of care, compassionate professionals try to see promise, potential, and the prospect of growth and change in fallible people.

Key Components

- *Value each person as worthwhile and inherently deserving of your assistance.*
- *Accept each person without condition or reservation.*
- *Listen carefully and work at understanding each person's experience.*
- *Discern ways to promote each person's well-being and alleviate suffering.*
- *Without discounting wrongdoing, offer grace and compassion even when client's let you down.*

47
Offer Pro Bono Service

A successful loan officer at the local branch of a major bank, Cindy had considerable expertise in small-business financing. As Cindy's professional and personal fortunes grew, she felt compelled to find some way to give back to her community. She derived some satisfaction from helping in a local food pantry and volunteering as a tutor in an elementary school. She knew she found her niche, however, when the head of a local association of aspiring minority business owners approached her for advice. She began offering pro bono services to the local men and women interested in launching their first business. Twice a month, Cindy attended the association's meetings, gave a short talk about some aspect of small-business financing, and then answered questions and shared ideas about approaching banks, managing books, and even how to locate potential investors. Not only did Cindy enjoy her time with the association members, she recognized that her work had a big impact. Without her assistance, many of the members would have failed in their business ventures. Cindy soon discovered that her pro bono service was one of the most meaningful dimensions of her work.

The compassionate professional's moral compass will always point in the direction of those who most need help. After all, compassion is a deep awareness of the suffering of people coupled with the wish to bring relief. We should keep in mind that the people who are most in need of professionals' help are the ones least able to pay for it. Due to the real needs of those who are less fortunate and unable to get professional services on their own, compassionate professionals offer a portion of their time to these individuals.

Many professions explicitly enjoin members to offer a portion of their work pro bono, or voluntarily and without payment, as a means of serving the underserved. The term *pro bono* is derived from the Latin meaning "for the public good." When professionals engage in volunteerism, three salient things happen. First, people in the community who might otherwise go without important professional help (e.g., medical care, mental health services, legal advice, financial counseling) have the opportunity to become "clients." Pro bono work alleviates individual suffering, improves the condition of the impoverished, and reduces the strain on public relief and welfare services. Second, the public image of the profession is enhanced. When physicians offer time to a homeless clinic, attorneys give a morning a week to advising low-income retirees, or a professional athlete waves a speaking fee when addressing a youth organization, these acts of volunteerism renew the public's faith in human goodness.

The third thing that happens in response to pro bono work is something intrinsic—professionals' self-satisfaction and personal fulfillment increase exponentially. Translating compassion into genuine service allows professionals to find a satisfying answer to Aristotle's piercing moral question: *In my professional work, who shall I be?* Beyond income, status, and power, who will I *be* in relation to my community and the population of human beings—many of whom are suffering—that occupy it? Pro bono work offers one compelling way of expressing care in response to human need.

In the context of your professional work, consider avenues for donating time and expertise. Although the exigencies of life and the realities of making a living will set a limit on how much pro bono work you can offer, chances are that allocating some time each day, week, or month to serving the needs of the underserved will benefit you just as much as it benefits the recipients of your work.

Key Components

- *Become attuned to local populations most in need of your services.*
- *Volunteer a portion of your time and professional expertise to those who could otherwise not benefit from your work.*
- *Ask yourself how you can contribute, who you wish to be, vis-à-vis your community.*
- *Remember that compassionate professionals promote the public good.*

48
Attend to More Than the Bottom Line

When Lonny was elected chair of the state psychological association's ethics committee, most psychologists in the state lived in fear of coming to the committee's attention. Historically, the ethics committee's primary mission was to hear complaints against members and levy severe penalties, most notably expulsion from the association. Lonny was appalled after attend-

ing his first meeting of the committee and observing how a few members ridiculed the judgment, intelligence, and character of the psychologists under review. He knew that this arrogance was being communicated to members of the association and that it had several dire consequences, including the failure to see the psychologists who had erred as fallible human beings, an overly harsh approach to sanctions, and the creation of an environment of contempt. The attitude also served to distance committee members from the uncomfortable reality that each of them had the potential to engage in professional wrongdoing of equal indiscretion. Lonny immediately confronted this behavior and reminded the members of the committee that the charge to behave with compassion and avoid harm applied to both clients and colleagues. The committee members took earnest heed of Lonny's admonition. As members' attitudes shifted, the general perception of the committee changed in the professional community. It became known for its outreach to impaired colleagues, efforts at prevention, and a graceful but firm approach to adjudication.

Never sacrifice a person for a principle. Never let the bottom line blind you to the human cost of achieving it. And remember that the lure of profit can diminish the strength of compassion.

The virtue of care demands that we recognize principles and policies as avenues for respecting and helping others. They must never be deified or valued above the rights and concerns of individuals. The ethical requirement of compassion is threatened the moment we objectify or neglect the dignity and worth of a person we lead or serve. We all know professionals who become so enamored of rules, so preoccupied with spreadsheets, or so self-righteous in meting out punishment that they lose sight of the human beings impacted by their dispositions.

Like Lonny's colleagues on the ethics committee, even ethics "experts," those populating the ethics committees of various professions, may fail to see the human forest through the trees of laws and standards. At times, adjudicative bodies lose touch with the reality of compassion when sanctioning a colleague who has erred. Ridiculing and demonizing another person for failure allows us to ignore our own frailties. In contrast, genuine compassion compels us to keep humanity in plain view. We should view ourselves and the people with whom we sit in judgment as humans—nothing more, nothing less. Loving those we serve, demonstrating care, and ensuring justice are evidence of attending to more than the bottom line.

Although successful CEOs often are depicted as ruthless cost-cutters, impervious to the lives of employees they fire by the thousands, the business world is taking a hard look at the moral and financial fallout of this approach. Business innovator John Elkington (1994) and other visionaries have proposed a moral framework for thinking about sustainable and ethical corporate profit. Elkington's *Triple Bottom Line* model defines a company's success according to people, planet, and profit. In this model, corporate leaders are accountable to their "stakeholders" including employees, community members, customers, and fellow inhabitants of the environment, not just "shareholders." When a CEO's company reaps a profit but simultaneously leaves employees and their families destitute or the environment diminished, Elkington asserts that this leadership without compassion will backfire in the long run. Ethical professionals demonstrate commitment to the welfare of employees and communities. They appreciate the powerful connections between promoting the welfare of employees, giving back to the community, engaging in sustainable environmental practices, and making profits. These leaders see all of these activities as mutually inclusive.

Key Components

- *Never let personal gain or financial profit blind you to the human and environmental impact of your work.*
- *Remember that rules and principles must serve the interests of human beings.*
- *Avoid ridiculing or demonizing colleagues who err.*
- *Show compassion, even when enforcing standards and delivering sanctions.*
- *Consider people and planet when calculating profits.*

49
Protect Vulnerable People

Robin was a district manager for a large custodial services company. She was keenly aware of the necessary tension between earning profits and caring for her employees. She was sensitive to the fact that many of the custodians she hired lived at or below the poverty line, lacked formal education, or were not fluent in English. Some struggled with disabilities, and most were no more than one paycheck away from financial ruin. Attuned to their many challenges, Robin took tangible steps to protect her employees as best she could. For instance, when headquarters threatened to make workforce cuts, she curtailed hiring and arranged attractive early retirement options for her most senior employees. Her intent was to avert layoffs. She hired a social worker to help employees find needed social services, financial counseling, and legal assistance. She was a stalwart advocate of company-sponsored educational opportunities, language courses, and junior management training. Over time, Robin's compassionate leadership paid huge dividends in the form of deeply loyal employees, stable families, low attrition, and the highest promotion rate into junior managerial jobs in her company.

The ethical life is thoroughly dependent on the virtue of care. When professionals respond to the needs of others out of affection and regard, caring is present. Mahatma Gandhi understood this phenomenon when he reflected that the best way to find yourself is to lose yourself in service to others. This virtue may best be framed as a form of love. It is an act of love to respond to the need or predicament of another person—especially when no one is looking. Such loving care fuels empathy, compassion, and a drive to protect those who cannot adequately protect themselves.

A key element of care is the willingness to make provision for or offer protection to those among us who are most vulnerable. Supporting people who, by virtue of age, circumstance, or distress, cannot fully care for themselves is the heart of professional compassion. Horticulturalist and educator George Washington Carver understood this principle when he wrote, "How far you go in life depends on your being tender with the young, compassionate with the aged, sympathetic with the striving, and tolerant of the weak and the strong—because someday you will have been all of these" (Carver & Kremer, 1991).

Who is vulnerable? Many factors can place individuals or entire groups at risk of poverty, neglect, exploitation, and acute suffering. Ethical professionals are alert to the unique vulnerabilities of children, the elderly, and persons struggling with physical or mental disability. Further, professionals remain sensitive to the myriad ways gender, race, religion, geographic location, and other personal variables can exacerbate vulnerability and suffering. Professionals with a highly developed sense of compassion rarely have difficulty noticing the human being who has been diminished by a personal trait or unfortunate circumstances. In fact, caring professionals easily might feel overwhelmed by the needs of those they serve.

How should we respond to the vulnerable people we encounter in our professional lives? As ways of expressing care, professionals may render any number of services—often pro bono—for the most vulnerable among us. Direct support might include financial relief (e.g., waived or reduced professional fee), access to information, advice and guidance, referrals to key resources, direct advocacy, and help with filing for assistance or making a complaint. Whatever you offer by way of direct advocacy and support for those in need, make an effort to be empowering versus demeaning.

Remember this: Taken to an extreme, even the virtue of care can become a vice. To the extent that professionals become paternalistic and controlling of vulnerable people, they may undermine their autonomy and perceived control. We call this phenomenon *intrusive care*. Intrusive professionals assume an air of superiority. They act like they understand people when they do not. They treat people with special needs disrespectfully, try to force them into decisions that really are self-serving, and further marginalize them.

Finally, learn to detect signs of maltreatment and abuse of vulnerable people. Then become familiar with laws and professional guidelines requiring you to report abuses. For instance, many states require professionals to file formal reports of suspected abuse of minors, elderly persons, and individuals with developmental disabilities. These groups are given special protections under the law, specifically because of their vulnerabilities.

Key Components

- *Be particularly vigilant to the needs of your most vulnerable clients, consumers, and colleagues.*
- *Remember that certain demographics and circumstances can put people at risk for specific types of suffering and vulnerabilities.*
- *Avoid intruding on the autonomy and independence of those you help.*
- *Pay attention to indicators of abuse or exploitation in vulnerable clients, and report these occurrences to appropriate authorities.*

7

Seeking Fairness

Matters of Justice

Ethical professionals treat others equitably. All of us not only must honor human rights, we indeed must protect the rights of others. We should consider it our obligation—morally, ethically, and professionally—to be just and fair in all of our dealings. We should regard the obligation as sacrosanct. Avoiding unfair discrimination, exercising reasonable judgment, and taking precautions to prevent personal biases from creating unfair outcomes are all ethical obligations that must remain entirely independent of personal attitudes toward any of the persons involved. Genuine fairness must be impartial and universal.

In this chapter of *The Elements of Ethics*, we emphasize those matters of ethical practice most relevant to justice and fairness. Ethical professionals are careful to give full credit to those who contribute to any task or product. They are explicit and open in communicating performance criteria so that subordinates and others understand what is expected of them. Ethical professionals discriminate fairly, and treat people equitably, which is not necessarily the same as treating them equally. They refuse to be complicit with unfair practices or policies, and they are judicious in balancing the competing demands of advocacy and gatekeeping.

50
Give Credit Where Credit Is Due

Not until she ran into the president did the lights come on at last. Not until then did Seunghee realize that Katrina, her manager for the past three years, had been keeping senior management abreast of Seunghee's innovations in the marketing department. Katrina was terse, exacting, and not particularly warm. She demanded results and rewarded them with more challenging assignments. For three years, Seunghee had been primarily responsible for some of the marketing department's most effective and innovative marketing campaigns. Sales were up, way up, but Seunghee had begun to wonder if Katrina was taking most of the credit herself—passing off Seunghee's best ideas as if they were her own. Seunghee's worries were erased on the elevator ride during which the president praised her achievements and lauded her creativity. He described some of her most notable ideas in enough detail that it became crystal clear Katrina had been very specific about Seunghee's contributions to each major campaign. The president further noted that he was seriously considering Katrina's recommendation that Seunghee receive a major promotion within the department. Whatever Katrina lacked in the area of interpersonal skill, she made up for in professionalism. Seunghee became one of Katrina's most loyal colleagues.

Stealing is a most despicable crime. Stealing occurs when someone, without permission, takes and keeps something that belongs to someone else. The stolen object can be anything that is not owned by the thief. We have special names for the wide variety of ways people steal: shoplifting, burglary, larceny, looting, mugging, embezzlement, trespassing, fraud, plagiarism, kidnapping, and rape. Although everyone knows stealing is wrong, the behavior is alluring enough that we have to pass laws to protect the rights of innocent victims and give out stiff penalties to deter thieves. The right of ownership underlies protection and determent.

Do you think stealing is not a problem among professionals? The federal government would beg to differ. A recent study by the FBI estimates that in the United States alone businesses lose nearly 300 billion dollars annually to white-collar crimes. While financial theft may be more egregious and clearly illegal, we all know professionals face numerous temptations to take things that do not belong to them. And much of what is stolen is not tangible property.

The moral virtues of justice (fairness) and integrity require us to truthfully represent our contributions to any work as well as represent others' contributions. The requirement infers that we must not claim or accept credit for work that is not ours. In applying the principle of ownership, failing to give credit where credit is due and taking credit where credit is not due, in effect, are acts of stealing. And the types of stolen property may include achievements, accomplishments, ideas, and contributions—anything that belongs to other people or results from their independent thinking and efforts.

Plagiarized work ranks high on the list of intangible stolen property. *Plagiarism* is the unauthorized use or close imitation of someone's language and thoughts while simultaneously representing them as one's own. Unauthorization and misrepresentation are the twin issues that make plagiarism an ethical problem. In addition, if the work is patented or copyrighted, plagiarizing it might be a crime.

What causes professionals to steal? Unchecked ambitions, arrogance, or desperation for recognition—these are the attributes of professionals who jump at the opportunity to take undeserved credit. And claiming undeserved credit can be subtle. Allowing a supervisor to believe that an idea or innovation is our own, rather than belonging to a subordinate, is just as unethical as plagiarizing an author's published work.

However, here is another side of the coin: Do not give credit where credit is *not* due. For instance, don't attempt to bolster students' or junior colleagues' careers by inflating your evaluation of their competence. Someday you will be called on to serve as a reference, and you might feel the subtle pressure to write a glowing letter of recommendation. Be careful. It is just as dishonest to make baseless recommendations as it is to steal someone's idea. Moreover, the dishonesty creates erroneous expectations, probably causing harm to the person given undeserved credit and the organization that hires the person.

Finally, take this advice: When working as a team member, have ongoing discussions about credit, authorship, or relative ownership. An informed and consensual process for allocating credit is both professional and ethical.

Key Components

- *Never take credit for work, ideas, or achievements that are not your own.*
- *Always give credit to others whose work you have used or benefited from.*
- *Have early and ongoing discussions with team members about relative contributions and appropriate division of credit.*
- *Do not give credit to people who have not made a significant contribution.*
- *Recognize that taking credit for a subordinate's work is a form of exploitation.*

51
Make Performance Criteria Explicit

After nearly three decades as an economics professor, Dr. Carter had mastered the art of mentoring graduate students. Early on in his career, he had learned the value of taking great pains to clarify what he expected from each new doctoral student. Typically, his expectations included hard work, the delivery of assignments and drafts of the dissertation on time, reliable assistance in his research lab, and the development of innovative research designs. He communicated these expectations in clear fashion verbally and in writing, and he reiterated them at key junctures during each student's career. Furthermore, he told students to notify him immediately if any of these expectations could not be met. His annual evaluations and his letters of recommendation always referred specifically to how his graduate students met each expectation. Although Dr. Carter's protégés found him demanding, they were immensely grateful for his fair and explicit approach to defining performance criteria. Other graduate students in the department were not so fortunate. They suffered with faculty who seemed unable or unwilling to clarify expectations. These students felt anxious, confused, and eventually angry when their evaluations appeared to be based on vague or hidden performance criteria.

Track and field, for the most part, is a fair sport. What separates it from some other sports is the unambiguous judgment of athletes' performance. Whoever runs the fastest, jumps the highest, or throws the shot put the farthest wins. While every sport accedes to the principle of fairness, the margin of error in judging performance is greater in some sports than in others. In sports like track, the margin of error is low because the performance criteria for athletes are clear and explicit. In other sports, the evaluation of performance sometimes amounts to a judgment call, allowing subjectivity and potential error. We all have witnessed questionable calls made by officials.

Establishing explicit performance criteria is an ethical mandate for every professional who is involved in the supervision or evaluation of subordinates. Subordinates deserve to know clearly what is expected of them, and they should not be expected to guess about your expectations. When human beings are uncertain about what they are supposed to do, when there is a lack of clarity about expectations, they experience what social psychologists call *role ambiguity*. Research reveals a number of side effects to role ambiguity, such as low job satisfaction, high tension, erosion of self-confidence, a sense of futility, turnover, and substandard performance. Role ambiguity generally makes us feel anxious and even helpless.

You must clarify your expectations of subordinates and clients at the outset of a professional relationship. Then you must be sure that they know up front the criteria by which they will be evaluated. Clarifying expectations has a number of benefits. Superiors have a better chance of making fair evaluations. They are positioned to help subordinates develop professionally. Evaluations should be timely, conducted periodically, and should be followed by helpful feedback.

Offering formative feedback helps reduce ambiguity and correct deficiencies before they erupt into major problems.

Setting clear expectations may pose a challenge for a variety of reasons. First, some professionals themselves are ambiguous about the most appropriate performance criteria. They simply don't know what to communicate. Second, some professionals have difficulty with communication. They don't know how to communicate their expectations. Third, other professionals simply don't give enough priority to this responsibility. They seem oblivious to their subordinates' distress. Finally, some professionals have motivations that are sinister. They may be motivated by hidden agendas such as secretly wanting a subordinate to fail or get into trouble. They may use hidden criteria or change performance criteria midstream in order to sabotage.

Clarifying expectations is ethically appropriate because it puts the best interest of subordinates and clients in first place. Such clarity spares individuals needless confusion, and it frees organizations from mismanagement. Fostering confident workers and well-managed organizations reflects favorably on the ethics of a professional.

Key Components

- *Clarify precisely how and by what criteria you will evaluate others.*
- *Provide performance criteria well in advance of any evaluation.*
- *Offer formative feedback whenever possible in order to allow subordinates opportunity to make corrections and improvements.*
- *Do not base evaluations on hidden criteria and in such a way that subordinates are disadvantaged or harmed.*

52
Discriminate Fairly

Assistant Professor Maria Mendoza found herself in a tight spot. During her first year of college teaching, the glaring reality of grade inflation caught her off guard. Students wrote poor teaching evaluations in two of her courses. Known as demanding and having high expectations, Professor Mendoza soon was to get another shock. Her teaching standards were not in line with those of other junior members of the faculty in her department. Easy grading standards had become the unwritten norm. Young professors knew all too well that the stakes were high for getting tenure. Grading easy meant a better chance of getting good course evaluations, and getting good evaluations meant a better chance of getting tenure. In this situation, the ethical challenge actually was twofold—discriminating fairly and not giving in to pressure. Against the advice of other young professors, she chose what she thought was the ethical high road. She refused to grade easy and perpetuate the idea that all students had to do was show up for class, hand in mediocre term papers, and con the professor with flimsy excuses for missing class. Ironically, by the end of her first year, she had become a favorite among advanced students. Although she was tough, the word among students was that her grading was fair and her courses were stimulating and thought provoking.

The word *discrimination* arouses strong emotions. Most citizens hate the thought of being identified as prejudiced, bigoted, or racist. It is a difficult indictment for most people to accept. But because of the long history of prejudice, bigotry, and racism in the United States, Title IV of the 1964 Civil Rights Act was enacted. Title IV prohibits discrimination in the workplace. Employers cannot use race, color, sex, religion, ethnic background, or national origin as a basis for discriminating against employees in hiring, placement, and promotion. Subsequent amendments have extended the prohibition to include handicapped people.

The type of discrimination for which Title IV provides protection is known as *unfair discrimination*—differential and unfair treatment based on irrelevant or arbitrary factors. There is another type of discrimination, though, which is *fair discrimination,* and ethical professionals should aspire to put it into practice. To discriminate fairly means to make personnel decisions in hiring, performance appraisal, placement, and promotion on the basis of one's ability to do a job and the quality of one's work.

As a professional, you make numerous decisions. You frequently may conduct performance appraisals, delegate tasks to subordinates, intervene in conflicts, give pay raises, select bids, assess the merits of proposals, critique ideas, evaluate the quality of programs, and set priority on organizational goals. And this list is only a small sampling. But despite the importance of our decisions, many of them turn out to be nothing more than judgment calls and subjective at best. Think about some of your recent decisions and the real basis for making them. Can you honestly say that the decision-making process always was objective? We should admit that many of our decisions contain a high degree of subjectivity. But we should never resign ourselves to total subjectivity, particularly when our decisions may have a significant impact on others.

Professionals must register fair discrimination in their decision making. The best way to do this is to gather as many of the relevant facts as possible, weigh them against each other, and, most important, establish criteria that differentiate the quality of performance. Recognize that any decision making that is not based on fair discrimination practices may be an abuse of power and result in harm. It is fundamentally unfair, and, ironically, discriminatory.

Key Components

- *Do not make any personnel decision based on arbitrary or irrelevant criteria.*
- *Engage in fair discrimination by making decisions based on job-relevant factors.*
- *Avoid allowing race, color, sex, religion, ethnic background, or national origin to influence personnel actions and decisions.*
- *Be vigilant for evidence of both overt and subtle forms of unfair discrimination.*

53
Treat People Equitably, Not Equally

A busy pediatrician in a rural community, Casey was known for providing pro bono services to a number of recently immigrated families from Mexico.

These families did not qualify for health insurance, and many of them had
to rely on low-paying work as laborers in local agriculture. Over time, Casey
learned that she had to flex her bedside manner, her financial arrangements,
and even her interpersonal demeanor in order to best serve these families.
For instance, she became more comfortable with hugs from the parents, ac-
cepting small gifts of food, and allowing minor barter exchanges (e.g., eggs,
produce, firewood) in exchange for her services. Quietly, however, she did her
best to make very generous estimates of the value of her clients' goods so that
she was confident they did not exceed—or in most cases equal—the actual
value of her services. An outside observer might have complained that Casey
did not treat all her patients equally, because the majority of them were pay-
ing her standard rates. But she felt confident that her special allowances pro-
vided equity between "the haves" and "the have nots." She made sure that
every patient received excellent care, personalized attention, and a financial
arrangement that was sensitive to his or her means.

Psychologist Derald Sue made an astute observation. As a leading authority on counseling minority clients, he insisted that the equal treatment of clients should not be the goal of counselors (Sue and Sue, 2002). Because there are prominent differences between groups of people and within groups of people, treating all clients equally misses the point. According to Dr. Sue, treating clients equally might mean discriminatory treatment, a point we made in the previous element. On the other hand, treating clients differentially may not imply discriminatory treatment. Because equal access and opportunity is the most important goal, counselors should use *differential* counseling techniques that are *nondiscriminatory*.

Although Dr. Sue was speaking specifically about counseling, the principle of *equity* has universal application. In chapter 3, we emphasized the importance of honoring human differences. We made the point that all people have a threefold identity based on their membership in the human race, a reference group such as their gender or race, and their own individuality. Now we want to take this idea a step further. We must not substitute the concept of *equal treatment* for *equitable treatment*.

The rhetoric of equal treatment is ambiguous. A word or phrase is ambiguous if it can take on multiple meanings. The phrase *equal treatment* in one instance can mean treating everyone exactly the same way. In this case, the equal treatment might be insensitive to how individuals are impacted by the treatment. We can offer a burly football player the same portion of food we feed an infant. Here we have treated them equally. But is the treatment fair? No! The phrase *equal treatment* in another instance can mean treating everyone differently. In this case, the treatment could be sensitive to the unique needs of individuals, and the outcomes of the treatment might be similar for everyone. In the above example, instead of the same portion we feed the infant, we can offer the football player a full-course spread. Here we have treated them differently. But is the treatment fair? Yes!

Equal treatment in its purest form implies doing the exact same things to and for all of our clients and consumers. Unfortunately, this policy is rigid, legalistic, and insensitive to the unique needs, interests, goals, and aspirations of individuals. By adhering to this principle, professionals correctly may be invested in doing what is right while simultaneously neglecting what is in the best interests of each individual, for everyone is unique and situated in a context. Here the professional's emphasis on equal treatment may satisfy legal requirements yet fall short of key ethical principles such as nonmaleficence, respect, beneficence, prudence, compassion, justice, self-reliance, fidelity, excellence, and sound judgment. By contrast, *equitable* treatment does not have to imply doing the exact same thing to everyone. It might in many instances. Fundamentally, equitable treatment is flexible, sensitive, and responsive to the needs of individuals. While a philosophy of "anything goes" is never acceptable, professionals who are equitable not only do what is right but also what is good for people. Using the language of Dr. Sue, they apply differential approaches that are nondiscriminatory.

Key Components

- *Emphasize the equitable, not equal, treatment of those you serve.*
- *Seek to further the best interests of each individual, tailoring interventions and services to his or her specific needs and circumstances.*

• *Remember that serving a client's best interests requires flexibility.*

54
Don't Be Complicit with Unfairness

Armando's promotion to vice president for human resources constituted a major career achievement. He was delighted to find himself in a position to advance the well-functioning and success of his company's 50,000 employees. However, during his second month on the job, Armando learned that the company's promotion rate for female managers was abysmal, far below that of comparable companies. As he began to interview female managers and those in upper management tasked with making selection decisions, it became abundantly clear to him that the leaders of the company were supportive of family-friendly promotion policies in principle only. For women who took any time off for maternity leave or child rearing, it was all but impossible to recover and continue a successful upward trajectory in the company. As a result, many of the most talented women exited the company early in their careers—often getting hired by competitors. Armando took his concerns—bolstered by carefully collected data—to the CEO. Although he met with some resistance at first, Armando's steady and unrelenting insistence that the company was practicing unfair discrimination resulted in several key policy changes and more equitable promotion rates for women.

Human behavior never occurs in a vacuum. Even behavior that seems remote or isolated is nested in a social context, a network of relationships and interactions among people. Obviously, some behaviors are random, onetime events. However, the reoccurrence of a particular behavior or pattern of behavior indicates an undeniable attribute of the social context. The behavior has some degree of social support, even when the support is not readily apparent.

Veteran journalists Anne Farrow, Joel Lang, and Jenifer Frank drive this point home in their powerful, eye-opening book *Complicity* (2005). The subtitle vividly captures the book's central message: *How the North Promoted, Prolonged, and Profited from Slavery.* We all know about the horrid history of slavery in the South. But the North's complicity with slavery is not as well known. For many years, the North was a silent partner with the South, invested and even dependent on the success of this atrocity. Slavery was part of the North's social contract, and its economy was inextricably intertwined with slavery.

Complicity suggests a partnership or cooperation in wrongdoing, and it usually is evident in tacit support of unfairness. Dr. Martin Luther King Jr. understood the dangers inherent in complicity. He once said, "Injustice anywhere is a threat to justice everywhere" (King, 1964). If metaphorically you stand by, close your eyes, turn a deaf ear, pretend that injustice does not exist, and do nothing, you are part of the problem. The essence of complicity is putting up no resistance to wrongdoing.

You must realize that it is just as ethically corrupt to be complicit with unfairness as it is to directly engage in unfair practices. Your silence, coupled with your inaction, makes you culpable; you have become an accomplice to the crime. As a professional, you cannot easily excuse yourself from the responsibility of combating unfairness and inequity. You must understand that not doing anything bears the same consequences as doing something overt and egregious.

Key Components

- *Refuse to remain silent or inactive in the presence of injustice.*
- *Scrutinize your professional context and be vigilant for unfair practices.*
- *Ask questions and raise concerns about apparent violations of human rights.*

55
Balance Gatekeeping with Advocacy

Cary found herself in a real bind with Jennifer. Although Jennifer had been a stellar student academically and a quick study during her practicum training in physical therapy, a number of red flags had begun to emerge over the years. As Jennifer's primary academic adviser, Cary often found

*herself intervening on Jennifer's behalf for episodes of anger and verbal out-
bursts that seemed unprovoked and certainly were unprofessional. Several
instructors and supervisors had complained about these behaviors over the
years. Jennifer seemed to have no insight about her mood problem and poor
impulse control. She often blamed others for instigating conflict or brushed
off her explosions as simple misunderstandings. Although Cary had counseled Jennifer multiple times, documented these interventions, and even referred Jennifer for mental health care, there was little demonstrable
improvement. When it came time for Jennifer to register for her final year
in the physical therapy program—the year precipitating a full-time intern-
ship and subsequent licensure—Cary informed Jennifer that she could no
longer support her candidacy in the program. Her recommendation was
that Jennifer withdraw from the program or a take a leave of absence to
commence long-term psychotherapy. Cary explained that she was obligated
to ensure that only students with the ability to function professionally and
without risk of harm—including emotional harm—to patients be allowed
to graduate with a professional credential. Cary could not in good conscience
allow Jennifer to independently interact with physical therapy patients,
even though over the years she had made every effort to help Jennifer get on
track.*

The human body is amazing. Elegantly designed and possessed by
exquisite functionality, this masterpiece of creation is remarkably
adaptable, promotes its own health, and engages in self-healing. One
way the body achieves health is through complimentary operations
in the bloodstream. On the one hand, red blood cells deliver oxygen
from the lungs to body tissue. These are the most common type of
blood cells, and they operate as the principal mode of transportation
of oxygen. On the other hand, white blood cells defend the body
against infectious disease. Whenever germs or infections enter the
body, the white blood cells—always alert to intrusion—mobilize
themselves quickly to fight off the foreign intruders. The complimentary functions of red and white blood cells are essential to the
body's health maintenance efforts.

Ethical professionals must also balance the dual requirements of
gatekeeping and advocacy. Both operations are inextricably linked
to the health of your profession and to the safety of those you serve.

This element of ethics is most relevant to those of us who teach, train, supervise, or credential new members of our profession. Just as the human body is designed to promote its own health, professionals are ethically bound to promote the welfare of their profession and the public. Most professions impose an ethical obligation not to graduate or license those who because of their incompetence or lack of ethical sensitivity would inflict harm on the consumers whom they seek to help (Kitchener, 1992). Turning a blind eye to a trainee's ethical or emotional problems may simultaneously endanger the reputation of your profession and the welfare of those served by your profession. For better or worse, professionals must balance the obligation of advocate and caretaker for fledgling professionals with the obligation to protect the profession's gates from dangerous or incompetent applicants.

Through this gatekeeping operation, professionals defend their guilds from infectious incumbents or intruders. Incompetence, corruption, psychological disturbance, disregard for the well-being of clients—these are the types of intrusions that cause havoc, hinder efficacy, and damage others. Individuals who possess these qualities are the kinds of intruders who should be rejected. Of course, most trainees and novice professionals will exhibit more benign traits including a commitment to excellence, integrity, emotional health, ingenuity, and genuine empathy for those they serve—these are the types of individuals who must be supported and encouraged en route to full membership in your profession.

From the highest-ranking leader to the newest member of any profession, each professional should promote the health, integrity, and reputation of the profession while simultaneously minimizing the risk of harm to the public. Each member of a profession should regard the dual operations of gatekeeping and advocacy as an ethical imperative.

Key Components

- *Do not shirk either stalwart advocacy or careful screening of trainees.*

- *Accept the ethical obligation to serve as gatekeeper for your profession.*
- *Protect the public from potentially harmful professionals through rigorous screening and credentialing efforts.*
- *Do not allow advocacy and support to trump honest assessment of a person's moral character and psychological fitness.*

8

Promoting Autonomy

Matters of Self-Reliance

E thical professionals respect the rights, dignity, and worth of all people. One way to express this respect is through a firm commitment to support those you serve in making fully autonomous and independent decisions. We must respect the right of our clients to make fully informed choices about their lives and the services they receive. These choices should be free of coercion or interference. We must respect the fact that our clients, students, customers, and anyone else we encounter professionally have the right to self-rule, and we must accept their decisions—particularly as they relate to our services and professional recommendations. Certainly, we ought to assert our professional opinions even when they do not concur with the opinions of those we serve. However, in the final analysis, our clients' important life decisions do not belong to us.

In this brief chapter, we offer four elements of professional ethics bearing on the moral virtue of autonomy and the importance of promoting self-reliance in those we serve. Ethical professionals respect clients' right to self-determination and independence. They provide information, expert opinion, and professional recommendations, but they refuse to encourage dependency or undermine responsibility. Ethical professionals are attuned to the fact that services may cease to be helpful to a client, and when this is the case, they recommend termination of the relationship or referral to another professional. Professionals promote autonomy by taking a client-centered stance defined by collaboration. They reject hierarchy in favor of collegial alliances. Finally, professionals must honor each person's right to make an informed refusal. Genuine respect for autonomy demands honoring clients' prerogatives to refuse our best advice.

56
Encourage Independence

A seasoned guidance counselor for a large suburban high school, Connie often juggled the roles of surrogate parent, sage adviser, and life cheerleader for students in their last two years. Because the district was affluent and most students went directly to four-year colleges following graduation, students often felt considerable pressure from parents, teachers, and peers to perform well and get into the "right" schools. Understanding that the college admission process was stressful, that many of her students were struggling with significant career questions, and that more than a few of them were afraid of disappointing their parents, Connie had many students who leaned heavily on her for practical guidance and emotional support. While sensitive to her students' angst and unconditionally supportive and encouraging of each one, Connie knew that her preeminent duty was to help students prepare to make their own decisions about careers, colleges, and life in general. To this end, she plied students with detailed information, patient guidance, and powerful messages of affirmation. Students quickly discerned that Connie was in their corner no matter what their post–high school plans. They discovered something else about Connie. She would not make any of their decisions for them. Although this was unnerving for some, all of Connie's advisees appreciated her determination to honor their fledgling independence.

In the Declaration of Independence, certain unalienable rights are held to be self-evident. Among these are life, liberty, and the pursuit of happiness. Collectively, these rights as identified by the country's founding fathers represent individual freedom and independence.

Whatever else you might do, respect the inherent freedom and dignity of each person you encounter. Ethical professionals honor autonomy, the right to *self-rule*, in those they serve. Respect for self-determination requires us to avoid exerting control or interfering in others' lives whenever possible. Encouraging—even celebrating—our clients' independence is a primary moral requirement. The essential question is this: How can I help ensure that my client will make an informed, personally responsible decision but one that is devoid of coercion and undue influence?

Encouraging autonomy begins with solemn respect for the privacy, self-determination, and inherent worth of all people. In our work, we must diligently support others in making fully independent decisions. Promoting autonomy requires us to help those we serve gather appropriate information and understand the likely outcomes of a course of action. But it also requires us to get out of the way once our clients are ready to make a decision. Moreover, we hold an ethical obligation to fiercely protect our clients' independence should other persons or organizations attempt to constrain or undermine it.

To honestly model respect for autonomy, start by honoring your own. For instance, do not allow clients or others to threaten or manipulate you. Do not allow an insurance company or any other third-party organization to place limits on the quality of your service. Do not allow any entity to prevent you from freely expressing yourself, as long as what you say is truthful, responsible, and serves the best interest of your clients. When professionals fail to protect their own freedom, it is difficult for them to encourage independence in others.

Encouraging independence can be hard for several reasons. First, some of us like to control people as much as we like to control things. The elements of your personality that contribute to your success as a professional (e.g., assertiveness, self-confidence, being proactive) can have a flip side. You might find it difficult to relinquish control, even when doing so clearly is in your client's best interest. Therefore, we must be sensitive to an insidious vulnerability: the need to rescue.

There are professionals—many of whom are in the social services professions—who have a need to be needed, a need to call the shots in someone else's life, a need to offer people a band aid instead of a cure. Sure it feels good. But rescuing is a problem: It undermines personal responsibility and independence, ultimately diminishing a person's freedom. The line between authentic caring and paternalism is thin. Do not cross the line. Do not assume that you have all the answers. Ethical professionals render professional opinions but balance them with an encouragement of clients' independence and self-rule.

Second, promoting independence can be difficult when clients make decisions that run counter to our professional opinion. Clients' freedom to choose can lead them to decisions that might drive us crazy. When we ask the question, "How could they do that?" we should be ready with the answer, "Because they are human beings with the right to self-rule." And don't forget that true independence has another implication. People have the right to relinquish or suspend their own autonomy should they decide that they are incapable of making an informed choice.

Third, promoting independence must be tempered with sensitivity to cultural differences. Cultures vary on the level of importance they place on independence, and the differences are most notable between traditional Western and Eastern cultures. Overemphasizing autonomy can conflict with respecting a client's decision to relinquish autonomy or self-interest, perhaps in favor of the interests of family, a religious community, or even a marriage partner. Be mindful that our unique experience of gender, race, ethnicity, and religion shapes our preferred balance of autonomy and interdependence. Don't force your own notions of "appropriate" independence on those you serve.

Here is one final caveat: While encouraging independence, be vigilant for signs of danger. Whenever clients pose an imminent danger to themselves or others, professionals have not only an ethical responsibility but often a legal responsibility to take appropriate action to prevent the threat of danger. Under these circumstances, contacting local authorities is the right course of action.

Key Components

- *Respect each person's dignity and worth by promoting independence.*
- *Support the right of others to make autonomous choices.*
- *Never encourage dependence or undermine freedom in those you serve.*
- *Respect the role of culture in clients' balance of autonomy and interdependence.*
- *Protect your own autonomy as a way of positive role modeling for others.*

57
Terminate Services That Cease to Be Helpful

Lloyd was a relatively junior physical therapist. The owner of his practice, he received referrals from surgeons and other physicians. He specialized in helping clients regain a full range of movement following injury or surgery. When one of Lloyd's favorite patients, a 70-year-old woman recovering from double knee-replacement surgery, failed to keep several appointments in a row, Lloyd followed up with a phone call to verify that she was OK. During the conversation, the patient admitted that she had not experienced significant pain for several months and that physical therapy no longer seemed necessary. Troubled, Lloyd checked her chart and discovered that the patient had been in therapy for more than 18 months—far longer than normally indicated. His own documentation revealed that the patient had reached maximum benefit from physical therapy within the first year. After some soul-searching, Lloyd was forced to admit that he had neglected to carefully assess his patient's progress and recommend termination or significantly reduced appointment frequency once most of her goals (e.g., pain-free walking) had been achieved. He was forced to admit that he had grown so fond of this patient that he had been inattentive to the normal treatment regimen and forgotten to encourage her termination of physical therapy when the time came.

Promoting autonomy requires the professional to discontinue services when it becomes reasonably clear that a client no longer is benefiting from or potentially may be harmed by them. Keeping a client in treatment, consultation, or any other service when it has ceased to be helpful violates the principle of autonomy. Unhelpful services also mean undeserved benefits to the professional. If you are benefiting more than your client (e.g., financially, emotionally), it is probably time to make a referral or terminate services.

Nothing can undermine a person's sense of autonomy like a professional who nurtures—consciously or unconsciously—a sense of dependency. Many of our clients already struggle with strong dependency needs. Their identity may be defined by a sense of inadequacy, self-doubt, and low self-esteem. The ethical professional recognizes signs of dependency in clients (e.g., hiding evidence of improvement, avoiding discussion of termination, pleading for direction) and slowly but adamantly requires them to assume more responsibility for their decisions and self-governance. If dependent clients show no evidence of improvement and self-reliance, professionals eventually must confront them with this problem. If change is not forthcoming, they must develop a clear plan for referral or termination. And remember that it always is unethical to use fear or other forms of coercion to keep a person in a professional relationship. Using one's positional power to manipulate a client (e.g., hinting that dire consequences may follow termination of services) who is ready to move on is clearly unethical.

So how do ethical professionals know when a client no longer requires services? They rely on formal assessment. They return to the client's reason for seeking their services in the first place and consider the client's improvement. During periodic reviews—a hallmark of ethical practice—they determine clients' progress. Has the rate of improvement leveled off? Is there any real evidence that significant change continues to occur? At times, our clients begin to offer indirect evidence that they are ready to terminate. Missing appointments, "forgetting" to complete assigned work, or rejecting our advice might mean resistance. But it could be an indicator that the client is ready to move on.

Professionals never should lose sight of the fact that they are both human beings and professionals. While their professional side is alert to strategies for promoting client autonomy, their human side can be reluctant to "let go," even when a client is not benefiting from the relationship. Professionals should examine themselves and see if any of these descriptions apply to their fostering of dependency in clients: (1) The professional who is struggling financially may overlook evidence that termination is in order; ending the relationship may create a financial strain on the professional; (2) roles may become reversed in the relationship so that the client has begun to meet the emotional needs of the professional; a dependent, narcissistic, or love-struck professional may work hard to keep a client coming back as a way of gratifying personal needs; or (3) the professional may lose sight of the client's goals and perpetuate the professional relationship as a way to coerce the client to adopt the professional's agenda.

When in doubt, professionals should get a second opinion. Consulting with another professional may shed light on confusing relationship dynamics and provide insight into a client's progress. A trusted colleague may help professionals identify their resistance to termination, unhelpful motivations for avoiding endings, or evidence that a client is indeed benefiting and will likely continue to benefit from their services. Consultation may strengthen a client's trust in the professional while helping the professional regain perspective on the client's best interests.

Key Components

- *Terminate services when they cease to be helpful to a client.*
- *Never use your power or expertise to coerce or scare a client into continuing in a professional relationship.*
- *Carefully assess client progress as a means of gauging the need for additional services.*
- *Get consultation if you are uncertain or conflicted about a client's need for continued services.*
- *Remain alert for evidence that your client is ready to terminate your services.*

58
Collaborate

When Virgil began practice as a clinical psychologist, he knew that his fa-
vorite part of his work was conducting psychological evaluations. He devel-
oped considerable expertise in testing and diagnosis and soon had a large
waiting list of clients referred by other professionals and attorneys. Clients
were sometimes surprised by the amount of time Virgil devoted at the outset
of an evaluation to asking the client what he or she hoped to gain from the
assessment, clearing up misconceptions, explaining the testing and inter-
viewing procedures he would use and how he would go about drawing con-
clusions from the results, and asking whom the client wished to receive copies
of the final report. By the time testing actually commenced, clients were clear
about what they were consenting to and comfortable with Virgil as a pro-
fessional. Furthermore, they were satisfied with Virgil's respect for their
rights and autonomy. When he assessed children, Virgil was equally deliber-
ate about putting them at ease, explaining the process in language they could
grasp and securing fully informed consent from their legal guardians.

If respect for autonomy is a fundamental ethical principle, then
few things express respect more powerfully than collaboration. The
collaborative professional works at forging alliances with clients, refusing to constrain clients' choices or dictate what is in their best interests. The ethical professional opts for a respectful partnership
aimed at achieving the client's goals, making no effort to deny his or
her relative power and expertise vis-à-vis the client, yet working patiently to establish a professional bond. Collaboration is an essential
indicator of respect for autonomy.

In all your endeavors, take a *client-centered* stance. A client-
centered approach is defined as proactive, inclusive, and cus-
tomized to the specific needs of those you serve. Collaboration
begins with sharing basic goals and understandings about the work
ahead. Share information freely with clients and take the time to
solicit and respond to their objectives and concerns. Respect for a
client's dignity and worth begins with really understanding his or
her unique frame of reference. Include clients in decision making

and work at making them feel like full-fledged partners in a joint endeavor. Finally, when appropriate—when requested by the client—collaborate equally with the client's family members, friends, and other professionals.

Client-centered collaboration hinges on trust, and there are few ways to strengthen trust more effectively than *informed consent*. Informed consent should illuminate clients' expectations and goals, the nature of the services and likely outcomes they can expect from the professional relationship, potential risks, their rights—including the right to withdraw at any time, financial and billing considerations, and anything else likely to help them make a truly informed and voluntary decision about entering and continuing in the relationship. Thorough and thoughtful informed consent involves a process of open communication and clarification. It is no surprise that some experts refer to this process as *empowered consent*. The goal is to provide clients with sufficient details about the road ahead. This information will enable them to give full and free informed consent. Deliberate informed consent also deters professionals from imposing their will unilaterally. Never assume that clients understand what to expect from you, and take the time to update the informed consent process as circumstances change.

How can the professional best collaborate, provide informed consent, and promote autonomy when the client's capacity for true autonomy is compromised? For instance, when engaging a person with limited cognitive ability, severe mental illness, or late-life dementia, or a minor who cannot legally give consent, think carefully about how best to collaborate under the circumstances. Even when a client is not capable of exercising full autonomy, the ethical professional endeavors to offer an explanation the client can understand, seek the person's assent, consider his or her preferences, and establish a collaborative relationship with the appropriate guardian.

Collaborate with clients whenever possible. When personal limitations or legal constraints prevent them from making meaningful autonomous choices, work with the client, legal guardians, and relevant systems to maximize autonomy and protect their best interests.

Key Components

- *Collaborate as a means of communicating respect.*
- *Focus on the client's concerns and objectives above all else.*
- *Provide thorough informed consent to enhance autonomous decision making.*
- *Protect the best interests of clients with diminished capacity for autonomy and collaborate with appropriate guardians.*

59
Respect Informed Refusal

Sonya had years of experience as an oncologist treating a vast array of patients with many forms of cancer. She was a tireless optimist about the potential for medical innovations to one day make cancer an entirely treatable disease. In her work, Sonya was aggressive in using combinations of chemotherapy and radiation intervention to combat even the most dangerous and incurable forms of the illness. Her patients and their families appreciated her upbeat and assertive tactics. She was forthright with them about their chances of beating cancer, even if the news was not encouraging. Nevertheless, her efforts nurtured hope, and many patients opted for the recommended course of treatment. Other patients opted to forgo treatment, preferring to enjoy their final months or years of life without the debilitating effects of medication and radiation—even though this meant abandoning any hope of prolonging their life. Over the years, Sonya learned to respect this decision and was graceful and supportive in providing end-of-life care designed to keep her dying patients engaged in activities they enjoyed for as long as possible with minimal discomfort. These patients and their families were deeply grateful for Sonya's thorough regard for their autonomy.

Respect clients' right to say no. True autonomy is impossible without the right to refuse any recommended procedure or intervention. *Informed refusal* is both a professional and legal concept. It is simply the right to reject any professional's recommended course of action. Assuming the person has an accurate understanding of the facts and the capacity to appreciate the implications of either consenting to or refusing a course of action, it is incumbent on the ethical professional to step aside and allow the client to decide.

Why is informed refusal such a hallowed ethical principle? Recall the infamous case of the U.S. Public Health Service (PHS) and the Tuskegee Alabama syphilis experiment mentioned in chapter 2. For 40 years, between 1932 and 1972, the PHS allowed 399 poor black men in the late stages of syphilis to believe they were receiving treatment for "bad blood," when in fact they received no active intervention, nor were they ever informed of the nature of their actual illness. The PHS was merely interested in studying the progression of the disease. None of these men, many of whom died from the ravages of syphilis or related complications, were aware they were participating in a government experiment. None were given the option to refuse. Like the physicians in Nazi concentration camps, the medical professionals involved in this experiment denied their "patients" a fundamental element of autonomy and human dignity—the right to say no to participation in an experiment or procedure.

Of course, full exercise of the right to refusal hinges on full informed consent. What is it about a recommended investment, diagnostic procedure, or long-term treatment that clients need to know before saying yes or no? What are the likely problems and sources of distress? What are the foreseeable gains and notable risks? Could undergoing this cancer treatment diminish the quality of a patient's last few months of life? Might embarking on intensive marital therapy result in a decision by a client's spouse to leave the relationship? Does this investment strategy carry the risk of a serious financial loss? Professionals demonstrate respect for others' autonomy by telling them everything they need to know to make a fully informed decision about participation or refusal.

In some circumstances, a client may not own the right to refusal. Professionals who work in special settings such as correctional facilities, mental hospitals, or the military may find that those they serve are *required* by law to undergo specific diagnostic or treatment procedures. Such contexts may present a moral/ethical dilemma for the professional. Here are the fundamental questions to ask: In light of this person's restricted right to refuse intervention, has the individual still been provided clear information about what to expect? Is the intervention likely to help rather than harm this person? Has everything possible been done to protect this person's privacy, dignity, and self-rule in light of the constraints of his or her diminished autonomy?

Provide enough information to the people you serve so that they can give informed consent or make an informed refusal.

Key Components

- *Always ensure that those you serve have enough information about a recommended course of action.*
- *Respect your clients' right to refuse participation in any activity or intervention.*
- *When circumstances limit a person's capacity to give informed consent or refusal, work with the system and any guardian to promote the client's best interests.*
- *Recognize that the right of refusal is a fundamental human right.*

9

Being Faithful

Matters of Fidelity

E thical professionals tell the truth and keep promises. They understand that honesty and promise keeping are fundamental to trust and that trust is fundamental to healthy professional relationships. The credibility and ultimately survival of most professions hinges on public perception. A professional's loyalty and trustworthiness go a long way in maintaining a profession's credibility. Being ethical means being faithful and honoring commitments. Inconvenience or difficult situations pose special challenges, but ethical professionals do not allow them to stand in the way of their commitments. When faced with an ethical conundrum, ethical professionals choose the course of action that permits the greatest fidelity to promises they have made. Although true fidelity necessarily entails some measure of self-sacrifice, a reputation for loyalty and promise keeping is priceless.

In this chapter of *The Elements of Ethics,* we cover four elements of ethics bearing on the principle of fidelity. Ethical professionals follow through with commitments and obligations, whether the obligations are to clients, colleagues, or other people with whom they have a professional relationship. They remain alert to conflicting loyalties and search for elegant solutions when possible. Professionals also appreciate not only current obligations but ongoing obligations inherent in certain types of professional relationships. These obligations are most notable in relationships involving a fiduciary commitment. Professionals give timely and honest feedback to those they serve, even when it congures up unpleasant feelings. The feedback should include a balance of positive and corrective observations, and without compromising accuracy, it should be delivered with sensitivity. Finally, ethical professionals actively support groups and organizations that regulate and monitor their profession. In their dealings with colleagues and regulatory agencies, they are cooperative and responsive.

60
Be Loyal

When Ray reflected on the early years of his accounting practice, he was amazed that he had managed to stay afloat financially and deeply grateful for those families and small businesses that stuck with him in spite of his novice status. They remained loyal to him through good and bad economic times. As his business prospered, Ray hired several more accountants. When a national accounting firm made a very lucrative buyout offer—one that Ray couldn't easily ignore—he agreed only on the conditions that he continue to personally serve each of his existing clients and that the same fee structure remain instead of the new one the company planned to implement. Although this national enterprise initially resisted Ray's conditions, a mutually agreed on arrangement was worked out. On learning of the agreement, Ray's clients were appreciative of his efforts on their behalf, but they were not surprised. Ray's faithfulness and follow-through were already rock solid. He was grateful for the opportunity to repay his clients for their loyalty.

For good reasons, dogs have been given the nickname "man's best friend." They are relentless protectors, life-saving rescuers, and demonstrate unsurpassed loyalty. On March 12, 2007, Lex, a German shepherd, sustained shrapnel injuries during combat in Fallujah,

Iraq. His injuries resulted from his refusal to leave the side of his handler, Corps Cpl. Dustin J. Lee, who was killed in the mortar attack. Lex later received a commemorative Purple Heart for his heroism. Who would not want a friend like Lex—someone who has your back even under the threat of death?

The ethical professional is faithful to commitments and obligations. Loyalty is synonymous with fidelity and implies a state of allegiance and devotion to those we serve, our colleagues, and our profession. To put it tersely, loyalty obliges us to do what we have agreed to do.

American writer Elbert Hubbard observed that an ounce of loyalty is worth a pound of cleverness. This sentiment flies in the face of the self-serving attitude common among many professionals. Fewer professionals exhibit loyalty to their company, organization, or even their clients when they are allured greater prestige or compensation that they can get elsewhere. But ethical professionals are loyal to those they serve and careful to honor commitments—even in the context of changing jobs. The moral virtue of fidelity demands loyalty even when loyalty is uncomfortable or inconvenient.

Loyalty is born of commitment. When a professional and a consumer freely enter into a relationship, the client is correct to assume a fiduciary commitment on the part of the professional to guard his or her best interests and remain loyal to the terms of the relationship. The informed consent process essentially becomes a statement of fidelity between the parties. It clearly identifies the requirements of both parties and defines the nature of the relationship. Now here comes the hard part: doing what we have agreed to do, even when we don't feel like it.

But loyalty comes with two caveats: First, a professional may occasionally struggle with *dual loyalty*—a situation in which loyalty to two separate interests creates a conflict. For instance, a physician's loyalty to a hospital or managed care company may at times conflict with his or her loyalty to the best interests of a specific patient. In such cases, the professional is ethically obligated to make the conflict known and to seek a solution that best serves the interests of all parties.

Second, indiscriminate loyalty is unacceptable because loyalty that does not meet certain criteria is not virtuous. In fact, under the wrong conditions, loyalty can be a vice. Consider blind loyalty to an unethical organization, an immoral institution, or an individual client who has violated the terms of the professional relationship. This is not the kind of loyalty found among ethical professionals. Be loyal, but show discretion.

Key Components

- *Be faithful to commitments and obligations.*
- *Keep promises to clients, colleagues, and your profession.*
- *Follow through with commitments even when doing so is unpleasant or inconvenient.*
- *Work to resolve conflicts born of dual loyalties.*
- *Remember that blind loyalty is not a virtue; some individuals and organizations are not worthy of loyalty.*

61
Assume Perpetuity

As a nurse in the mental health unit of a Veteran's Administration Medical Center, Melanee gave people effective counsel and reassurance. Kind, competent, and fun to be around, she was especially helpful to traumatized combat veterans. She listened as they told their stories of horror and described their painful memories, helping alleviate the intensity of their post-traumatic stress symptoms. Because she lived in a relatively small community, she frequently encountered patients outside the hospital— including many who had achieved significant improvement and no longer sought mental health services. On more than one occasion, she was tempted to accept an invitation from a former patient to attend a social gathering or go on a date, or to accept part-time employment as a home health nurse. On these occasions, Melanee simply reminded herself that it was not at all uncommon for her patients to experience relapses, to reenter treatment, and to once again rely on her professional care. To remain faithful to her primary role with patients, she politely refused these overtures and reminded

her patients that she always would be available should they again require
care at the VA Medical Center.

Some things in life—such as seeking safety, living healthily, and providing for one's physical needs—are nonnegotiable. These behaviors should be routine, life-long patterns. To negotiate or compromise on these behaviors is irresponsible and self-destructive. Similarly, fidelity to relationship commitments—including the obligations implied in some professional relationships—should never be negotiable. Although professionals may be tempted to skirt the implications of such enduring obligations, to do so is unwise—even dangerous—both for professionals and those they serve. When it comes to fidelity, there are no shortcuts.

Quite often, the provision of a professional service carries the implication of *perpetuity*. In a nutshell, the relationship with a client or consumer is considered everlasting. Once professionals enter a relationship as a service provider, they have no statue of limitations on certain obligations inherent in the relationship.

Why adopt such a long-term view of your role with clients? There are several reasons. The most pressing is the fact that fiduciary relationships—those in which you accept the trust and confidence of others to act in their best interest—obligate you to maintain your professional station vis-à-vis the client. Should you compromise your professional role or pursue an additional role with a client (e.g., social friendship, romantic relationship, business partnership), in effect, you more than likely eliminate the possibility of fulfilling your fiduciary commitment. Assuming that all professional relationships exist in perpetuity, even when the active phase of the relationship has ended, will go a long way toward reducing ethical slipups and unnecessary harm to clients who might one day again have need of your professional services.

The issue of perpetuity has garnered most attention in relation to postservice sexual and romantic relationships. Here is the quandary: Is it ever appropriate to terminate a professional relationship for the purpose of initiating a romantic liaison with a former client, patient, or student? Most professional organizations wisely outlaw sexual relationships with current consumers but place on the professional the burden of proving no harm when it comes to relationships with those formerly served. In addition to compromising one's fiduciary role, there are several reasons why taking on nonprofessional roles with former clients is unwise. First, like it or not, there will be an implicit power imbalance in the relationship. Those you serve as a professional will always accord you some measure of positional authority. Second, clients often reveal sensitive information in the course of professional relationships that may make subsequent social interactions uncomfortable. Third, there is a genuine risk of exploitation when a professional opts to meet social or sexual needs through a former client. This relationship may never be entirely mutual or freely chosen by the client. Research in academic settings indicates that even those students who are initially positive about romantic relationships with faculty members later report feeling diminished by the experience.

Here is the bottom line: Becoming a professional means eliminating the possibility of nonprofessional relationships with those you serve. Think of professional obligations to clients, patients, and other consumers as sacred vows. You must accept fiduciary responsibility for clients' best interests even when you have not seen the client for some time. Does this sound unfair? In some cases, it might be unfair. However, the high-stakes risks outweigh the dangers of dismissing this obligation. It is one of the costs of being a professional.

Is it ever possible to commence a nonprofessional relationship with a former client or consumer without causing harm or committing an ethical violation? Of course, it is possible. But all things considered, it is preferable to just say no.

Key Components

- *Begin each professional relationship with the assumption that your client will be a client in perpetuity.*
- *Accept that fiduciary responsibilities to clients are enduring, not temporary.*

- *Recognize that the addition of nonprofessional roles can confuse clients and undermine your professional effectiveness.*
- *Remember that professional relationships always involve a power differential and the risk of exploitation—even when not intentional.*

62
Provide Honest Feedback

A tenured professor of biology at a private liberal arts college, Charlene enjoyed teaching, advising, and mentoring promising undergraduate students. One of the aspects of her work she least enjoyed was giving students feedback about their career plans. Yet, Charlene felt strongly that giving honest feedback and serving as gatekeeper to the profession were ethical and professional obligations. As chair of the premedicine program at the college, Charlene was responsible for screening students prior to the medical school application process. Based on grades and test scores, a sizable portion of students each year who aspired—or whose families aspired for them—to attend medical school clearly were not qualified. Charlene met with each premed student several times during his or her first three years in the major and gave unvarnished but supportive feedback about the probability of medical school admission. Using objective performance indicators, Charlene kindly but clearly informed many students that their chances of gaining admission to medical school were not good and encouraged them to consider other career options. Although the feedback was difficult to hear, most students later reported appreciation for Charlene's candor.

Henry David Thoreau observed that it takes two people to speak the truth—one to speak it and one to hear it. Communication of truth, then, is incomplete without the active participation of both speaker and listener. Nowhere is this maxim more relevant than in the provision of feedback. But the process begins with the person giving the feedback.

Providing clear feedback to clients, students, and colleagues is an essential component of professional life. It is not simply criticism in disguise. Helpful feedback lets others know how effective they are, what is working, what is not working, and how they might improve their situation or outcomes. Constructive feedback can be reinforcing as well as corrective. The most effective feedback prepares the recipient for better performance in the future. If we are ethically obligated to promote the best interests of those we serve, then giving honest and helpful feedback is a key component of ethical functioning.

Fidelity requires honesty. It is hard to be faithful when faithfulness demands telling an unpleasant truth. Yet professionalism mandates the timely delivery of accurate, honest, and corrective feedback. When professionals give feedback that is insufficient, dishonest, or vague, and, worse, when they withhold feedback altogether, they fail one test of fidelity. Some professionals who withhold corrective feedback may fear they will embarrass or demean the person. Others may be passive or lack good role models for delivering effective feedback. Whatever the rationale, such neglect constitutes a compromise of one's professional role.

Ethical feedback will be facilitated by each of the following recommendations: (1) Be candid and honest; remember that the truth is liberating—even when unpleasant; (2) be supportive and considerate in your delivery; warmth and positive regard go a long way toward making corrective feedback palatable; (3) plan feedback intervals in advance so that feedback is integrated into the relationship from the start; avoid impulsive or emotion-fueled feedback; (4) be clear and specific; helpful feedback focuses on tangible behaviors and events; (5) integrate positive feedback into the process; frequent reinforcement makes occasional correction much easier to receive; (6) conclude each feedback session with a written summary and clear progress plan; such clarity can prevent misunderstanding; (7) finally, do not delude yourself with the belief that a significant problem will "just go away" without corrective feedback.

So how do some professionals bungle the feedback process? There are myriad ways to undermine the efficacy of your feedback efforts. Feedback that is abrasive, attacking, demeaning, publicly humiliating, vague, exclusively critical, impulsive, or indirect is unlikely to help and may actually diminish the functioning of those you are obligated to serve. When a professional withholds positive feedback, enjoys criticizing, or offers critique with no suggestions for improvement, the consumer is undermined.

Give honest and timely feedback. Make sure correction is laced with strong doses of reinforcement. And make feedback part of each professional relationship from the start.

Key Components

- *Tell clients the truth about what works well and what needs improvement.*
- *Use both reinforcement and correction to help those you serve.*
- *Be honest and sensitive in delivering feedback.*
- *Weave feedback into the professional relationship from the start.*
- *Provide specific feedback and offer tangible steps for achieving improvement.*

63
Actively Support Professional Regulation

Nels was shocked and anxious when he became the focus of an ethics complaint during his second year of practice as an audiologist. Feeling that the complaint—regarding his billing practices—was frivolous, he initially was noncompliant with the state licensing board's efforts at investigation. This resistance led to a formal hearing with the board in which he was reprimanded soundly for failing to uphold his responsibility to his colleagues and his profession. He also was reminded of the fact that failure to cooperate with an ethics investigation was itself an ethical violation. Although the complaint was eventually dismissed, the experience created a lasting impression on Nels. He realized that membership in his profession implied a clear ethical obligation to uphold the highest standards of practice and to fully support efforts at professional regulation and discipline. To make good on his renewed professional commitment, he joined the state audiologist organization, volunteered to supervise unlicensed professionals, and eventually was elected to serve on the state licensing board. Nels confronted colleagues when unethical behavior was exposed and came to appreciate the vital importance of transparency and cooperation in protecting both the public and his profession.

Formal relationships, especially those that are legally binding, carry explicit responsibilities that bracket those relationships. The ethical principle of fidelity goes beyond loyalty to clients and consumers. It also demands faithfulness to one's colleagues and profession. Professionals must support professional regulation and take action when the behavior of a colleague is in error.

A profession's very survival hinges on the ability of its membership to effectively control admission and hold members accountable to specific practice standards. The granting of licensure or admission to a professional organization implies a willingness to comply with specific rules, standards, and ethical practices. Unless professionals see themselves as part of a community of colleagues—each dependent on the ethical compliance of the others—fidelity to professional standards is difficult to achieve.

As a professional, you must uphold standards of conduct, clarify your ethical obligations, accept responsibility for your behavior, and confront colleagues who fail to do the same. The public perception of your profession and the protection of individual consumers are at stake. When it comes to safeguarding your profession's image and promoting regulatory efforts, be an active leader.

Why do some professionals fail to cooperate with regulatory bodies? There are several reasons. Some professionals become immobilized in the face of a complaint. Like deer in headlights, they may engage in denial or fear self-incrimination should they cooperate. Some professionals allow anger at the complainant or the regulatory body, their own defensiveness, or a stubborn belief that "frivolous" complaints require no response to stymie appropriate cooperation. Whatever the explanation, remember that failure to fully support the efforts of licensing boards, ethics committees, and other legitimate regulatory bodies constitutes an ethical violation. Don't allow your anxiety or indignation to sabotage your professionalism.

How can you actively support professional regulation? Here are several recommendations:

- Always cooperate fully with any ethics complaint or investigation—even if you have reason to doubt the veracity of the complaint or the intent of the complainant.
- Be thoroughly familiar with the ethical standards of your profession and relevant laws governing practice in your jurisdiction.
- Remember that regulatory bodies do not expect perfection but merely that you meet the standards of your profession in abiding by practice guidelines and ethical standards.
- Don't allow your own shock or emotional disturbance about an ethics complaint to prevent a timely and cooperative response. Seek legal and collegial consultation when appropriate.
- Be alert to unprofessional or unethical conduct in colleagues and, when appropriate, work to bring about an informal resolution to the problem (e.g., consultation, encouragement, provision of information).
- When these informal strategies fail or when there is a likelihood of substantial harm to clients or organizations, file a formal complaint with the most appropriate regulatory body.
- Strongly consider volunteering for service as a member of a professional licensing board, ethics committee, or other regulatory body. Such service often strengthens commitment to professionalism.

Key Components

- *Be transparent and cooperative with regulatory bodies in your profession.*
- *Remember that the expectation of fidelity and loyalty extends to your colleagues and your profession.*
- *Hold yourself and your colleagues accountable to current ethical and professional standards.*

- *Keep emotional reactions in check when responding to a complaint or confrontation by a colleague.*
- *Actively participate in professional organizations and serve on regulatory boards when the opportunity arises.*

10

Delivering Your Best

Matters of Excellence

Mediocrity, shoddiness, and unreliability are unacceptable in the performance of ethical professionals. Most of us can identify people whose work habits do not measure up to high standards. They may put in the time but not the needed effort. They pretend to work hard but hardly work. They make much to do about their capabilities but have little to show for what they have done. In this chapter of *The Elements of Ethics*, we devote attention to matters of excellence. *Excellence* is the state or quality of being good to a very high degree. Excellent professionals adhere to ethical principles with distinction and notable virtue. An abiding commitment to deliver one's best is a hallmark of the ethical life. To deliver their best, professionals must demonstrate certain behaviors. They must excel on the fundamentals and refuse to settle for legal compliance. They must stay in their professional lane, and they do not cut corners.

64
Excel at the Fundamentals

Although Mark never considered himself an academic whiz or a management "guru," he would admit that he had done well in his career as a

business leader. He had advanced from a junior manager position to be-
come the CEO of a major midwestern food company, along the way win-
ning numerous awards for running a company that employees
consistently rated as one of the best places to work in the country. When
colleagues probed him for the secrets to his success, Mark often surprised
them with his very direct and seemingly simple reply: "I excel at the fun-
damentals." By this Mark meant more than foundational business prin-
ciples. He also meant fundamental rules of human engagement and
ethical practice. He would elaborate, "I have worked hard to be kind, com-
petent, honest, reliable, and fair. My employees have rewarded my com-
mitment to these fundamentals with their loyalty. I am certainly no Wall
Street business genius, but I do treat those who work with me the way I
would want to be treated, and this has made all the difference."

Kihon is a Japanese word meaning "basics" or "fundamentals." The
term is used in reference to the basic techniques found in the teaching and practicing of martial arts. Included in the basic techniques
are stances, punches, kicks and blocks, cuts and thrusts, and *kata*, detailed choreographed patterns of movements. The mastery of *kihon*
in the martial arts is a prerequisite for proficiency and advanced
training. Complex actions depend on mastery of the fundamentals.
Winning a black belt in karate without first mastering the basics is
impossible, for discounting *kihon* is like trying to build a house without laying a foundation.

Fundamentals are the foundation of excellence. As in the mastering of *kihon* in the martial arts, excelling in fundamentals is a prerequisite for proficiency as a professional. To master fundamentals,
one must practice relentlessly. There is no substitute for time and effort when developing professional excellence. But practice itself is
not enough. You must engage in accurate practice. Basketball super-
star Michael Jordan put it this way: "You can practice shooting eight
hours a day, but if your technique is wrong, then all you become is
very good at shooting the wrong way. Get the fundamentals down
and the level of everything you do will rise" (Lowe, 1999).

Of course, every profession or vocation has its own fundamentals.
We might say they are profession-specific fundamentals. These are
knowledge, skills, and attitudes essential to professional practice.

Gourmet cooking, cattle ranching, detective work, aviation, bio-chemical engineering—each has its unique knowledge base and skills, setting it apart from every other profession. You have to train in the profession to discover them. Yet the fundamentals of ethical excellence apply across professions.

What are the fundamentals of ethical excellence? The elements in this book include fundamental obligations that cut across the professions. Still, some facets of ethical excellence might be considered more fundamental than others. Legendary basketball coach John Wooden describes five core fundamentals in his "Pyramid of Success." At the foundation of his pyramid lie industriousness, friendship, loyalty, cooperation, and enthusiasm. To this noble list, we would add several additional basic building blocks including integrity, working to help and not harm others, honesty, showing respect, demonstrating compassion, maintaining a healthy mindset, and responding thoughtfully when ethical conflicts arise.

Key Components

- *First, focus on your fundamental ethical obligations.*
- *Practice integrity, compassion, fairness, and other ethical fundamentals before worrying about your profession-specific obligations.*
- *Practice the ethical fundamentals across time and situations.*

65
Do Not Settle for Legal Compliance

José often referred to them as the "lunch crowd," colleagues at the community college where José was an instructor. Unfortunately, the lunch crowd were in the majority. They were complacent, somewhat lazy instructors who, having achieved tenure, showed up to work only when they had to teach, rarely published anything, and were often scarce when students needed basic advising—let alone good mentoring. The lunch crowd pursued a minimalist agenda. They tried to work as little as possible, planned their weeks around long lunches, and spent considerably more time griping about their pay and talking about retirement than actually aspiring to great work in the classroom. José and a few prized colleagues refused to capitulate to pressure from the lunch crowd to bring their work ethic down to this level. José worked long hours focused on teaching excellence and responsive advising. He sponsored two student organizations and was the department chair in his discipline by default—none of the senior instructors were willing to do any extra administrative work. José believed that it was both a moral and ethical duty to aspire to excellence in his professional work. He understood that the academic and even life success of his students was at stake.

Legalistic Leroy—we all have run into him and seen how he operates. He does what he must but nothing else. His mode of operation is legal compliance, whereby minimal standards of performance become his maximum standards. Do not expect him ever to go beyond the call of duty. Do not expect him to find novel ways to make a contribution. Do not expect him ever to do more than what is required. His behavior is so bureaucratic and he is so legalistic about following the rules that he never extends himself, never offers new ideas, never provokes rethinking of operational strategies, and never challenges the status quo. He just puts in his time and collects his paycheck.

Consider how Leroy behaves when proposals for change are put forth. He opposes them out of hand, probably because change is a threat. After all, he is in a comfort zone. Change just might force him to yield on his bureaucratic behavior, move beyond his comfort zone, and stretch himself. If his resistance is not overt and direct, he behaves as a passive resistor. On the surface, he might appear to support a proposal for change but not so in reality. You can detect his resistance by the conspicuous absence of his constructive suggestions or his withholding of requested insights related to the proposed change.

Leroy is shrewd. You can't bring him up on charges of an ethical violation. But you still can question his ethics. He would never violate organizational rules and policies or violate the rules of his profession's code of ethics. But where he does not violate the letter of the law, he falls short on the spirit of the law. Ask him to lend a helping hand, and he would be quick to answer, "That's not my job."

Maintaining high standards and promoting the interest of their organizations are ethical principles professionals should value highly.

For instance, the Code of Ethics of the American Psychological Association states: "Psychologists strive to maintain high standards in their work" (APA, 2002). Nowhere is a commitment to excellence more evident than in a professional's approach to continuing education. Because the knowledge base in most fields is ever expanding, and because our professional training quickly degrades and becomes obsolete over time, it is incumbent on professionals to actively and consistently update their professional competence. There is a great difference between reluctantly earning just enough continuing education units to comply with credentialing requirements, and actively working to expand one's knowledge in the field and sharpen one's competence as a matter of professional pride and accountability.

Although legal compliance is not an ethical violation, just getting by, doing only what is required and nothing more, and never promoting the best interest of your organization do not reflect positively on a professional's work ethic.

Key Components

- *Never settle for minimum professional requirements.*
- *Aspire to embody the highest standards of your profession.*
- *Place the best interests of those you serve first, even when this is demanding and inconvenient.*
- *Go the extra mile to ensure and maintain your professional competence.*

66
Stay in Your Lane

Monique was both hardworking and caring in her role as parole officer for a large metropolitan police force. The men and women whose cases she managed knew they could count on her to be there for appointments, to have high expectations, to hold them accountable, and to pursue them doggedly if they ran afoul of their parole guidelines. Because the city's social service system was in such profound disarray, it frequently was difficult for parolees to find affordable health care, good legal assistance, and other vital professional services. Bright and well versed in many areas, Monique was often tempted to recommend over-the-counter medical treatments, specific legal strategies, mental health interventions, and even tax advice. But she recognized that there was a fine line between offering well intended lay-person advice and practicing another profession without a license. She frequently reminded herself to "stay in her lane," meaning that she limited her professional work to reviewing and monitoring the terms of parole and offering encouragement and support in the form of appropriate referrals and practical advice.

Critically acclaimed author Pope Brock's book *Charlatan* (2008) dramatizes the serious consequences of professionals veering outside their lanes. The book details the disturbing and mind-boggling true story of a man who not only practiced outside the scope of his expertise but also gave the term *flimflam* new meaning. "Dr." John Brinkley, as he called himself, first sold worthless patient remedies. Then he moved on to the more lucrative and reprehensible practice of treating virility by transplanting goat glands into impotent men. Over the years, he harmed numerous patients, many of them dying at the hands of his quackery. America's most dangerous huckster, as Brock called him, made millions of dollars in the 1920s and 1930s until he was finally brought to justice.

Excellence as an ethical imperative requires that we limit our work to those areas in which we are competent—by virtue of education, training, and experience—to practice. We stay in our own lane, as it were, as a means of protecting others from incompetence and possible harm. Although we may be less likely to see people as outlandishly fraudulent as the charlatan Brinkley, there are plenty of professionals who veer dangerously out of their established areas of competence. They masquerade themselves as possessing competence they do not have. Occasionally, we may encounter someone who fraudulently claims to have certain educational and professional credentials, or who practices *pseudoscience*. Like Brinkley, they have no scientific or reasoned rationale for the services they offer. More often, we encounter individuals who are professionally trained and have legitimate credentials, and yet they step outside the bounds of their competence, delving into specialties or even professions for which they are not trained.

So let's be clear: No one has infinite knowledge or boundless expertise. Without question, omniscience and omnipotence are not human qualities. Therefore, in respect of their humanness and out of the desire to do their very best, professionals should put brackets around their abilities. They need to respect where their competence begins and where it ends.

During your career, you will undoubtedly encounter pressure or temptation to practice outside the bounds of your competence. You must never yield to this temptation. Even if your professional organization has no formal code of ethics bearing on boundaries of competence, never masquerade as someone with a competence you do not possess. Stand ready to demonstrate that you have been driving in your own lane.

Key Components

- *Know the boundaries of your own competence and stay within them.*
- *Never practice in specialty areas or in other professional domains without appropriate education, training, and experience.*
- *Resist the temptation to make recommendations that a different sort of professional should be making.*
- *Stay in your professional lane as a way to protect those you serve.*

67
Do Not Cut Corners

A newly minted school psychologist, Taren was pleased to receive a job offer from a small private practice group that specialized in conducting evaluations for learning disabilities and other educational problems in children. Within her first few days on the job, however, Taren began to have serious misgivings. A perusal of the testing supplies revealed outdated and even obsolete assessment tools. In some cases, the materials were a decade out of date, and the group had failed to invest in the more recent, well-researched versions of these instruments. The testing materials clearly were not the standard in the profession, and Taren knew that many of the older versions were not normed appropriately for children from different cultural groups. Furthermore, many of the newest and cutting-edge assessment tools—now the gold standard in the field—were not included in the testing materials. When Taren brought her concerns to the attention of the group's primary partners, she was informed that purchasing new materials was too expensive and considered frivolous. She politely explained her ethical concerns with using obsolete materials for such high-stakes testing and cordially resigned from her position.

On August 1, 2007, a bridge on Interstate 35-W in Minneapolis collapsed, plunging 13 people to their deaths in the Mississippi River below and injuring 100 other people. Investigators from the National Transportation Safety Board later were shocked by the revelation that undersized gusset plates had been used in the bridge's construction. According to Chairman Mark Rosenker, the plates were about half the thickness required. Once the plates were incorporated into the completed bridge, they were beyond the detection of inspectors. The blueprints for the bridge were never located, making it difficult to know whether the design error was an unintentional oversight or a deliberate effort to cut costs. Regardless of the cause of the design flaw, this tragedy reminds us of the potential danger of cutting corners.

Cutting corners has many faces. Here are a few examples: using paid time to work on personal projects, failing to correct errors in our work when these are brought to our attention, showing up late for work and leaving early, employing outdated or obsolete techniques, rushing through difficult tasks so as to undermine the quality of one's outcomes, using inferior materials, and covering up shoddy work. The common denominator in these examples is the delivery of work that is not commensurate with expectations or even the standard in one's field.

Cutting corners is predicated on dishonesty and deception— dishonesty because it's a misrepresentation of the truth, deception because the intent is to hide the misrepresentation. *Dishonesty* is verbal or nonverbal communication stating a quality of work that in actuality does not meet expectations. *Deception* is deliberate action intended to imply that expectations have been met. On the surface, the work may appear acceptable, even outstanding. Below the surface lies a different story. The purpose of cutting corners is to accrue undeserved benefits, sometimes in the form of less work, sometimes in the form of more profits, and sometimes in the form of higher status.

Professionals who cut corners always exact some adverse consequences. At the very least, they have to protect the misrepresentation from becoming public. Sometimes the corner cutting manifests itself in the inadequacy or failure of products, goods, or services. In any case, exposure of the corner cutting sheds light on the professional's inappropriate behavior.

In stark contrast to cutting corners stands the behavior of someone like Honest Abe. A man of impeccable integrity, Abraham Lincoln never cut corners or sold short his patrons. His nickname befit his character. Here is how biographer J. G. Holland (1998) described him:

> He could not rest for an instant under the consciousness that he had, even unwittingly, defrauded anybody. On one occasion he sold a woman a little bill of goods amounting in value, by the reckoning, to two dollars and six and a quarter cents. He received the money, and the woman went away. On adding the items of the bill again, to make himself sure of correctness, he found that he had taken six and a quarter too much. It was night, and closing and locking the store, he started out on foot, a distance of two or three miles, for the house of his defrauded customer, and delivering over to her the sum whose possession had so much troubled him, went home satisfied. On another occasion, just as he was closing the store for the night, a woman entered, and asked for half a pound of tea. The tea was weighed out and paid for, and the store was left for the night. The next morning, Abraham entered to begin the duties of the day, when he discovered a four-ounce weight on the scales. He saw at once he had made a mistake, and shutting the store, he took a long walk before breakfast to deliver the remainder of the tea.

The old saying is as relevant today as ever: "Honesty is the best policy." Professionals must deliver excellence by refusing to cut corners, or otherwise benefit from substandard work and subsequent efforts to hide their duplicity. Ask yourself if there are areas in which you cut corners. If so, consider the Lincoln model, and seek to make amends.

Key Components

- *Refuse to cut corners or take shortcuts in your professional work.*
- *Remember that ethical excellence demands aspiring to the highest standards of your profession.*
- *When errors or mistakes become evident, correct them if possible and make them known to anyone likely to be adversely impacted.*

11

Making Ethical Decisions

Matters of Sound Judgment

Decisions! Decisions! Decisions! Life is full of decisions. In every area of life and throughout our careers, we face the challenge of making important and often difficult decisions. Some of our decisions have long-term or life-altering consequences, while others appear comparatively inconsequential. Whether the decisions we face are major or minor, there are two unalterable elements to ethical decision making. First, ethical excellence hinges on the practice of sound judgment. Second, arriving at a decision most likely to benefit those served requires a deliberate decision-making process. The best decision-making models involve a series of thoughtful and sequential steps. Much like a preflight checklist in the hands of an experienced pilot, a good ethical decision-making strategy helps professionals avert ethical errors.

Good judgment, discretion, and sound decision-making processes are nonnegotiable elements of ethics for professionals. The utilitarian argument that the end justifies the means simply must not influence your ethical deliberations. Whether you are a corporate president or kindergarten teacher, the mandate to employ sound judgment in professional decision making applies. Indeed, most professional ethics codes require members to employ a process of intentional deliberation and discretion in arriving at any ethical course of action.

In this chapter, we focus our attention on the process of ethical decision making—a topic too often overlooked in the literature on professional ethics. Our aim is to help readers better understand the intricacies of the decision-making process. To that end, we make the case that ethical decision-makers engage in a number of activities. They study the ethics code of their professions. They distinguish ethics from morality. They understand the nature of ethical concerns and differentiate these from ethical problems. They make every effort to prevent ethical concerns from becoming ethical problems. They creatively solve ethical problems, recognizing that overly simplistic solutions usually understate the complexity inherent in many ethical quandaries. Finally, thoughtful professionals seek collegial consultation when confronting complex ethical challenges. These activities culminate in professionals' employing a coherent model of ethical decision making.

68
Study the Ethics Code of Your Profession

Fresh out of graduate school and newly minted as a veterinarian, Yvette was eager to launch her career. She joined an established veterinary medicine practice and soon was building a loyal clientele of pet owners. To her surprise, several ethical situations emerged during her first few months on the job. They concerned the care of terminally ill animals and some of the practice's billing procedures. Having recently completed her professional ethics course in vet school, Yvette quickly revisited the relevant sections of her profession's code of ethics, which she used as the basis for bringing her concerns to the attention of her colleagues. Her collaborative, positive manner proved itself a major factor in change. She helped her colleagues understand the ethical issues entangled in their practice, but her collaborative style helped minimize their defensiveness. In her first year, she worked with her associates to modify informed consent documents, client billing procedures, and animal-care protocols. Although a few of her colleagues jokingly

referred to Yvette as the "Ethics Czar," the nickname actually was an affir-
mation of her professionalism. During her many years of employment at the
clinic, not one ethics complaint was brought against the practice.

Most professional associations have a code of ethics. These carefully crafted documents provide principles and standards of professional conduct. In general, *principles* are aspirations (ethical ideals),
while ethical *standards* are more specific (often enforceable) regulations bearing on the professional's work. The intent of these codes is
to provide clear guidance or ethical rules of the road. Think of your
profession's code of ethics as distilled wisdom, guidance imparted by
more seasoned practitioners. Ethics codes serve to protect the public
from ethically inappropriate behavior and protect professionals from
straying outside the boundaries of appropriate professional conduct.
Of course, ethics codes also serve as a means of holding professionals accountable for their actions. The word *accountable* is important.
Professional associations recognize the dangers inherent in sponsor-
ing professionals who lack accountability. Ethical standards help reassure members of the public that professionals will act in their best
interests.

An important premise underlies ethical codes. Practitioners of
the respective professions ultimately are responsible for knowing
and abiding by their professional code in the course of their day-to-
day practice. The responsibility never lies on the shoulders of consumers, clients, patients, or other recipients of professional services.
For instance, professional psychologists are responsible for maintaining appropriate boundaries with clients in therapy. Although a
client may develop a sexual attraction toward the psychologist and
may even initiate conversation about physical intimacy with the psychologist, the psychologist is the one who is ethically bound to prevent an actual sexual relationship. The ethical buck always stops
with the professional.

Finally, keep in mind that your profession's ethics code is a document to be honored both implicitly and explicitly. Don't settle for
minimal compliance or defensive practice. Defensive professionals
ask this question: "What do I need to know in order to protect

myself from malpractice lawsuits or ethics complaints?" In contrast, proactive professionals ask themselves these important questions: How can I uphold the highest standards of my profession's code of ethics? How can I take steps in advance to prevent harm to my consumers? How can I maximize the probability that my clients will benefit from their engagement with me?

Know and honor your profession's code of ethics. Be grateful for the wisdom it imparts, and seek to express its principles and standards in all of your professional activities.

Key Components

- *Know your profession's ethics code inside and out.*
- *Consistently work at expressing these principles and standards in your work.*
- *Use the ethics code to promote positive practice, not defensive self-protection.*
- *Make yourself accountable to your code of ethics.*
- *Recognize that adhering to your code of ethics enhances the public perception of your profession.*

69
Distinguish Ethics from Morality

Josh, an Army psychologist on his second tour of duty in the Middle East, encountered a difficult ethical situation when some of the men and women in uniform presented serious anxiety disorders, especially post-traumatic stress disorder (PTSD). A good number of these combatants were on their third or even fourth deployment, and many had been diagnosed with PTSD during previous tours. Josh began to feel a sense of moral outrage. To him, the prospect of sending these impaired soldiers back into active combat after only cursory assessment and treatment was unjustifiable. Then he began to wonder if sending anyone into harm's way was fundamentally unethical. Josh shared these concerns with a seasoned supervisor who helped him separate his firm moral convictions about the sanctity of life from the ethical obligation to help and not harm. Josh was reminded

that he did not have the power to decide which combatants returned to ac-
tive duty, only the power to provide good care and make recommendations
to superior officers. In this context, Josh's moral convictions likely would
find greatest expression in staying engaged, providing excellent care, and
making honest recommendations to commanding officers. In spite of his
objections and inner conflict, Josh realized that inaction and withdrawal
would probably cause more harm than good to the men and women he was
ethically bound to serve.

Many people mistakenly use the terms *ethics* and *morality* inter-
changeably, assuming these words have the same meaning. Consequently, they also use their corresponding adjectives *ethical* and *moral*
without making a distinction between them. The perpetual inter-
change of these words creates confusion. And the confusion hinders
the ability of professionals to execute best ethical practices.

How then is ethics different from morality? Before we answer
that question, we should note that the two words have something in
common. Both are concerned with behavior. *Behavior* is psycho-
motor activity—what people do. Professional behaviors cover a wide
range of activities such as making phone calls, typing on a computer,
delegating responsibility, creating financial budgets, and making
ethical decisions. By definition, behavior always leads to some outcome, a consequence. When professionals make a decision, the decision will impact the decision-maker, other people, and possibly an
entire organization. This definition of *behavior* has an important
implication: Although it may be counterintuitive, taking no action
is itself a behavior. Passive inaction has consequences. At times, the
results of inaction may be profound for professionals, clients, and
possibly an entire community. Keeping the definition of *behavior* in
mind is essential to understanding ethics and morality. Let's explore
the differences.

Morality or its variant, morals, pertains to general or universal
principles of human behavior. These principles are not bound by
time, location, culture, race, or gender. Human dignity, solidarity, and
social justice exemplify the types of principles that are valued univer-
sally. Endorsing universal principles is one thing. Putting them into

practice is yet another thing. The reality is that morality does not exist in a vacuum. It requires a social context that gives the universal principle practical meaning. This is where ethics comes into play.

Ethics refers to the interpretation of general principles of morality within a specific context. The codes of ethics of professional organizations illustrate this point. Demonstrating support for human dignity may be reflected differently in the actions taken by attorneys, medical doctors, and teachers. A defense attorney may argue that there is insufficient evidence that an indicted client is guilty of a crime. A physician may recommend high dosages of morphine for a patient dying of cancer. A teacher, on seeing a student struggle with reading, may lobby for a careful assessment of learning difficulties.

There is another distinction between morality and ethics. Moral principles are not only universal, they remain constant over time. The principle of social justice is just as relevant today as it was centuries ago. Historical records and personal experiences demonstrate numerous violations of the principle, but the principle of social justice endures the test of time. On the other hand, ethical standards often change over time and context. As professional organizations and other social groups reevaluate their ethical codes and apply them to the myriad ethical problems they encounter, old ethical guidelines give way to new standards. The reevaluation and revision of codes of ethics is apparent in all professional organizations.

Morality and ethics are distinct aspects of professional excellence. But they also complement one another at every turn. Our moral convictions guide and inspire us to the highest ethical ideals. Think of moral virtues as the bedrock or framework for ethics, and think of ethics as the expression of our moral commitment in tangible professional behavior. Morals and ethics are distinct, but they always are intertwined and essential for professional excellence.

Key Components

- *Understand morals as universal and timeless principles of human behavior.*

- *Understand ethics as the interpretation and expression of moral principles in a specific context or profession.*
- *Recognize that moral principles and ethical standards are distinct but intertwined; ethics emerge from moral principles.*
- *Expect professional ethics to shift and develop over time in response to emerging professional challenges.*

70
Investigate Ethical Concerns

Rumors were flying. Jean and John were the talk of their Chicago-based consulting firm, the subjects of titillating gossip. Jean was an attractive, twenty-something project manager, who recently was selected for early promotion. John was her 40 year old supervising manager. The two were seen on occasion working after hours, and they were known to travel together on business trips. In the rumor mill, it was said that their relationship was more than collegial, that John was granting Jean special privileges, and that Jean's promotion was not merit based. Was this a case of office romance fueling unfair favoritism? Selena, a colleague of John's, wasn't convinced. She remembered what it was like for her, just out of college and young, gifted, and assertive. She also knew what it was like to experience jealousy from colleagues, especially older men who wanted to feel superior and other women who wanted to attribute her success to personal moral compromises. Selena went to Jean and John privately, told them what the gossip mill was producing, and was relieved to get the real story. Jean's training in bio-engineering, coupled with her business acumen and savvy, put her at the forefront of some cutting-edge technology. Senior management wanted to capitalize on Jean's knowledge and John's leadership. So the principals of the firm had asked the two to team up, and quickly ramp up a first-in-its-class service before the competition got wind of the plan. The very nature of the project required that many of the details remain strictly confidential.

Mental health researchers Paul Watzlawick, Janet Beavin, and Don Jackson (1967) tell the story of a man who collapsed and was rushed to the hospital. The attending physician was very concerned about the man's unconscious state, his extremely low blood pressure, and the clinical impression of acute intoxication. However, lab results revealed no traces of chemical substances in the patient's system. The physician was unable to explain the condition until the man regained consciousness. At that point, the man explained that he was a mining engineer who recently returned from working for two years in a copper mine located in the Andes mountains. The altitude of the mine was 15,000 feet above sea level. It now became clear that the patient's condition was not the result of an organ or tissue deficiency. Instead, it involved the adaptation of a healthy individual to a drastically changed environment. If medical professionals had limited their focus to the overt symptoms, failed to dig deeper into the patient's biochemistry, and overlooked the ecology of the patient, a potentially serious misdiagnosis could have occurred. Remember this: Any apparent problem will remain a mystery if the context in which the apparent problem occurs is not taken into account.

An ethical concern arises when questionable professional conduct, a potential lapse in integrity, or possible conflicts of interests come to a professional's attention (Ridley, Liddle, Hill, & Li, 2000). A concern may register as subtle unease or disturbing disquiet. Investigating an ethical concern is like observing a person who manifests some disturbing physical symptoms. You have reason to believe there might be a problem, but you need to understand the context and gather more information to decipher what really is going on. Rushing to judgment at this stage may amount to ethical misdiagnosis and perhaps even malpractice. Therefore, raising an ethical concern is not enough. Professionals must investigate the concern. The investigation requires a twofold process: gathering data and evaluating the data. First, you gather as much information as possible, frame the concern in its context, and determine the nature of the interactions between the individuals involved. Second, you carefully put the data in perspective. Evaluating the concern is tantamount to making an accurate, impartial, and comprehensive ethical diagnosis.

Before embarking on an investigation, we should familiarize ourselves with the three key components that constitute an ethical concern. First, an ethical concern is defined by the words *questionable* and *possible*. Not all questionable professional conduct results in substantiation of ethically inappropriate behavior. Because there is smoke does *not* mean *necessarily* there is fire. Second, an ethical concern should spur us to ask probing questions and talk to the professionals who are involved. We must avoid the temptation to look the other way and take the path of least resistance. Most ethics codes enjoin professionals to be proactive in addressing ethical concerns. But simultaneously we must be humble and not rush to judgment. Sometimes the concern amounts to nothing more than misunderstanding or misinformation. Third, an ethical concern signifies a deliberate and respectful process. A colleague's behavior may be *under consideration* during the time required to explore the facts and engage in a process of discernment. The purpose of the discernment process is to determine whether or not the concern is a potential or actual problem. One of three outcomes may result from the process: a determination that no ethical problem exists, a determination that a potential ethical problem exists, or a determination that an actual ethical problem exists.

Overlooking an ethical concern is not an option. We always should seek to investigate the circumstances concerning a potential or actual ethical problem. Failure to investigate an ethical concern makes the professional complicit if the concern is really a problem. Failure to investigate a concern also may contribute to its exacerbation as an ethical problem: The longer it remains unresolved, the worst it gets.

Key Components

- *Be alert to ethical concerns, but take the necessary time and steps to get the facts.*
- *Remain alert to the context of a professional's behavior; get the whole story.*
- *Remember that ethical professionals bring ethical concerns to their colleagues' attention.*
- *Be respectful and use discernment when exploring ethical concerns.*

71
Prevent Ethical Concerns from Becoming Ethical Problems

"What in the world is going on around here?" That was the question on Ben's mind. The first physician's assistant to join the large and vibrant internal medicine practice, Ben had been enjoying his work and getting to know the doctors on the staff. But Ben became alarmed on noticing that the medical practice was billing his services to insurance companies and even Medicare under the regular physician code. At first he thought there must be some mistake. He wondered if his imagination was running wild. His fears were confirmed when the secretary in charge of billing acknowledged that she had been directed to use the physician code. The rationale given was that "the insurance companies reimbursed at such a low rate to begin with." Although he knew that these practices were not uncommon, he also knew they were unethical and illegal. Not wishing to draw the ire of his new boss but fearful of the consequences of this breach of ethics, Ben decided to share his concerns privately with the head physician. Rather than hurl accusations, Ben gently outlined his concern about the inaccurate billing codes, explained how the practice violated his ethics code, and asked that the billing records be amended and the policy corrected at once. The chief physician agreed wholeheartedly, admitting he had paid little attention to this issue. He appeared relieved that a potential ethical/legal nightmare had been averted.

In late May 2007, federal health authorities in the United States averted a potential health crisis. Using a private plane, the Centers for Disease Control and Prevention (CDC) flew a man diagnosed with a dangerous strain of drug-resistant tuberculosis from New York to Atlanta. On arrival, CDC officials served the man with an isolation order and put him under federal quarantine at Grady Memorial Hospital. Plans then were made for the man to undergo surgery and drug therapy to kill the infection. Having determined that eminent danger loomed on the horizon, the CDC took this rare and decisive action. If the man remained untreated and continued normal contact with other people, a drug-resistant tuberculosis epidemic could have been imminent.

The decisive action of the CDC is a facsimile of the action principled professionals should take. When they are confronted with ethical concerns that either have the potential of becoming ethical problems or already may be ethical problems, the last thing they should do is nothing. The next to the last thing they should do is act slowly or indecisively. Because of the high value they place on ethics, professionals ought to be concerned with the prevention of ethical problems, that is, keeping ethical concerns from becoming ethical problems. Of course, an ethical concern does not automatically signal an ethical problem. Professionalism requires a willingness to explore concerns. An effective discernment process, as noted in the previous element, should be undertaken.

Ethical concerns that seem serious raise a number of questions, such as: When does an ethical concern become an ethical *problem?* How do professionals determine whether an ethical concern is an actual or potential ethical problem? What action do professionals take if they discern that an ethical concern is indeed a potential or actual ethical problem?

Many ethical concerns may translate into little more than misunderstanding or a rather harmless oversight. The potential risk to any consumer or to the profession is minimal. We become more alarmed and more inclined to identify an ethical problem when the processes of understanding and discerning reveal a likely breach of integrity. As clear evidence of an ethically inappropriate behavior or a conflict of interest—particularly one prone to harm others or compromise the integrity of professional practice—emerges, we have an increasing obligation to address the problem either directly with our colleague or indirectly through formal committees or licensing agencies.

Remember Benjamin Franklin's popular saying: "An ounce of prevention is worth a pound of cure." Embedded in the saying is the realization that solving a problem before it occurs is the best solution. This admonishment is as applicable to the ethics of professionals as it is to every other area of life. Trust your professional instincts, and actively explore concerns about the ethical climate in which you practice. Address your concerns with colleagues, organizations, and consultants as a way of reducing the possibility that serious ethical problems will occur. Just be sure not to rush to premature judgment.

Key Components

- *Remain attuned to unease or disquiet about ethical behavior—both your own and that of other professionals.*
- *Be vigilant for ethical problems related to failures in integrity and the potential for harm.*
- *Appreciate the fact that not all ethical concerns translate into real ethical problems; therefore, do not rush to premature judgment about an ethical concern.*
- *Be persistent and direct but cordial and professional in exploring ethical problems.*
- *When possible, address concerns as a way of thwarting problems.*

72
Do Not Oversimplify Ethical Problems

House of Representatives delegate Lillian Diaz became the target of a public and hostile accusation of accepting election contributions that exceeded limits for organizations. Her accusers were a group of state delegates from the opposing political party. The local newspapers had a heyday with the accusation, and they all but tried and convicted Diaz in the court of public opinion. In accordance with protocol, a state ethics panel was formed to investigate the accusation. The panel's chairperson was a seasoned delegate and someone with a reputation for fair dealing and diplomacy. Although the preliminary evidence was incriminating—there were canceled checks from several representatives of one corporation—and although the House and the public were demanding rapid action, the chair insisted on slowing down the investigation. He was not surprised to discover that there was more to the situation than first met the eye. The corporation's donors had written personal checks, and it was unclear that Diaz's staff could have made the connection between them and the company. Also, there was evidence that the company deliberately attempted to sidestep the donor-limit rules. Finally, the investigation revealed that the company previously had used a similar strategy with several other state delegates—including some of the very people who had accused Diaz so stridently. When the panel held a news conference summarizing their findings and revealing the complexity of the problem, none of the original accusers were on hand.

Staff writer for the *New Yorker* Malcolm Gladwell authored the best seller *The Tipping Point* (2002). The subtitle of the book, *How Little Things Can Make a Big Difference,* hints at the inherent complexity of many problems in the world and the corresponding need to find simple *tipping point* answers in the midst of confusion and confounding circumstances. What he implies here is an axiom fundamental to all problem solving: Simplify puzzling problems without oversimplifying their complexity.

In chapter 1 of his book, Gladwell relates the story of the mid-1990s epidemic of syphilis in the city of Baltimore. Experts offered three different explanations. The Centers for Disease Control and Prevention asserted that the subtle increase in the severity of crack cocaine was the culprit. John Zenilman, an authority on sexually transmitted diseases, explained the problem as a breakdown of medical services. Bureaucracy and budgetary constraints forced a drastic reduction in personnel and outreach. John Potterat, a leading epidemiologist, argued that the demolition of high-rise public housing and abandonment of row houses caused a dispersion of crime and infectious disease to other parts of the city. No longer was the problem confined to a specific region of the city.

Gladwell acknowledges the merits of each of these explanations. Each contributed to our understanding of the epidemic. However, he challenges us with a more compelling and thought-provoking perspective on the problem. The epidemic reflects the interaction of all of these scenarios, and none of them alone adequately explains the problem. This is what he says:

> There is more than one way to tip an epidemic, in other words. Epidemics are a function of the people who transmit infectious agents, the infectious agent itself, and the environment in which the infectious agent

is operating. And when an epidemic tips, when it is jolted out of equilibrium, it tips because something has happened, some change has occurred in one (or two or three) of those areas. (Gladwell 2002, pp. 18–19)

Many ethical problems, like the epidemic of syphilis in Baltimore, cannot be reduced to lightweight analyses. It is easy to apply shorthand, oversimplified solutions to complex problems—problems that by their very nature have many components and interactions among the components. For instance, unethical billing practices may stem from a combination of misinformation, efforts to avoid exhausting red tape, and simple greed. An inappropriate sexual relationship may be motivated by loneliness, genuine affection, lust, and client transference in the therapeutic relationship. Plagiarism may be the outcome of several factors including laziness, an honest oversight, pressure to publish, or our intentional attempt at exploitation. In a nutshell, many ethical problems owe their existence to multiple causes.

Resolution of complex ethical problems is not a job for the faint of heart. It tests the wits of even the most astute professionals. Out of necessity, we first should gather as much information as possible. Second, we must think deeply and analytically about the problem. And third, we should get consultation on particularly difficult problems.

Key Components

- *Remain sensitive to the complex nature of many ethical problems.*
- *Avoid assuming a simple or single cause for any ethical problem.*
- *Allow the complexity of ethical problems to keep you humble and cordial in your interactions with those who appear to have erred.*

73
Resolve Ethical Problems Creatively

As a prison chaplain, Toby discovered early on that he had his work cut out for him. Protecting his "clients'" confidentiality was an audacious ordeal.

On many occasions, inmates would reveal facts about previous crimes, details regarding guard abuses, and eyewitness accounts of crimes committed between prisoners. Toby understood the centrality of confidentiality to his role as chaplain, counselor, and religious confidant. The pastoral counseling code of ethics required strict adherence to the principle of confidentiality. Toby was shocked to discover that the state prison system did not recognize his clients' right to confidentiality—even in conversations with clergy. Prison protocol specified that all employees were required to report confessions, facts related to crimes, and other details. State guidelines also gave the warden and his staff access to all chaplain counseling records. Rather than react impulsively, Toby undertook a careful and cordial campaign of consultation, consciousness raising, and conversation with prison officials. He cogently articulated the ethical conflict prison rules created, was cautious to document only the bare essentials of counseling sessions, and gave each of the inmates he counseled a clear picture of the limits on confidentiality. He simultaneously worked to earn the trust of prison officials. As a result, they became less intrusive and more prone to trust Toby to disclose any information germane to keeping prison staff and inmates safe.

When an ethical concern reveals an ethical problem, how should we respond? What is the best approach to solving the problem? If the problem defies an elegant solution, how can we minimize its effects? Creativity, flexibility, and innovation must be brought to bear in order to solve many ethical problems.

An ethical problem is usually more than a simple dilemma. In fact, the term *dilemma* often is used inappropriately. The word is Latin from Late Greek dīlēmmat. The prefix *di-* means "twice." This indicates a choice between two equally unfavorable alternatives. Of course, many ethical problems are quite complex, and rarely do we find only two alternatives or potential solutions. Framing ethical problems as dilemmas may perpetuate a kind of dualistic either-or thinking that actually becomes a barrier to creative problem solving. The first step in creative problem solving is to keep all options open.

A second facet of creative problem solving involves a willingness to work at informal resolutions whenever these are possible. Most ethics codes require professionals to make every effort to solve problems informally and collegially before escalating the situation to a formal ethics charge or complaint. Each of us carries the simultaneous obligations to protect the public, police the ethical functioning of members of our profession, and treat one another as we would like to be treated—as valued colleagues. To achieve these ends, we must not ignore evidence of malpractice or ethical wrongdoing in others. Yet, we must assume that most professionals do have moral scruples and regard for professionalism. Always assume that colleagues will be responsive to clear but kind feedback and correction. Calmly and clearly explain your ethical concerns, and offer to help your colleague find an appropriate solution to the problem. When various efforts at informal and collegial resolutions are not effective, then more formal intervention through adjudicative bodies may be required.

Finally, recognize that some ethical problems simply defy perfect solutions. For instance, professionals working in and through organizations may discover seemingly intractable contradictions between their ethical obligations (e.g., maintaining strict confidentiality) and the organization's policies (e.g., making certain records available for scrutiny or review without the client's permission). In these situations, ethical professionals make the ethical problem clear to all those involved, emphasize their commitment to the relevant ethics code, and then work collaboratively to resolve the problem. Clearly, a professional's most creative, innovative, and collegial skills will be demanded in such contexts.

When vexing ethical problems arise, remember that a jury of your peers may one day review your actions. In evaluating your actions, your colleagues may ask, "Did you do everything in your power to solve the problem creatively such that the best interests of those involved were most likely to be served?"

Key Components

- *Refuse to frame ethical problems in either–or terms.*
- *Accept that some problems will defy elegant or perfect solutions.*
- *Be creative and flexible in trying to find informal solutions to ethical problems.*

- *Recognize that conflicts between ethics and organizational demands are common, and they require your consistent best efforts at workable solutions.*

74
Employ a Model of Ethical Decision Making

Ruth had been a CPA for more than two decades. During that time, she experienced a lot of trial-and-error learning and nowhere more dramatically than through ethical and professional quandaries in which she found herself. They could arise anytime and anywhere. Early in her career, Ruth had a tendency of making knee-jerk decisions. It didn't matter whether she discovered a client or colleague engaged in dubious accounting or made an ethical blunder. As she matured and became more astute in these matters, her tactics became more deliberate. By the time she had become an executive at her accounting firm, junior accountants frequently approached her with questions or quandaries related to professional ethics. Ruth had become a master at helping these accountants slow down the process, reflect on the key ethical issues, explore the relevant dimensions of the ethics code, consider the best interests of clients, imagine the likely outcomes of various courses of action, and seek appropriate consultation from subject matter experts. Her thoughtful and reflective procedure was both reassuring and instructive to her protégés. It was no coincidence that accountants in Ruth's division received the fewest number of ethics complaints in the firm.

Ancient Greek playwright Sophocles said, "Swift decisions are not sure." The saying implies a danger in decisions that are not made deliberately and thoughtfully. Avoid snap decisions and impulsive actions when navigating ethical quandaries. Recognize that ethical concerns and problems often rear their heads just when your professional life is most frenetic. Your calendar is packed, the phone is ringing, you have reports to write, your desk is swamped, and suddenly you become aware of an ethical blunder, a colleague's transgression, or, worse, that you have been named in a complaint. For obvious reasons, you will need to have a clear decision-making strategy in place before such quandaries or crises arise.

Can't you just rely on your profession's ethics code to reach the appropriate solution to ethical problems? The answer frequently is a resounding no. Ethics codes are essential for providing guidance, identifying standards of professional conduct, and holding professionals accountable. But knowledge of an ethics code often is not enough to ensure ethical behavior. These codes rarely provide the *thinking tools* required for analyzing and resolving many of the unique problems professionals encounter. There are several limitations to most ethics codes, including: (1) Some issues cannot be handled merely by turning to a code of ethics; (2) sometimes our clients' interests are not fully protected by these codes; (3) ethics codes occasionally conflict with laws or regulations; and (4) no ethics code can conceivably cover the full range of professional settings and novel ethical quandaries you are likely to encounter; new concerns and problems always are emerging.

To avoid rigid and oversimplified application of an ethics code, professionals must employ a deliberate strategy for slowing down the decision-making process. Specific steps and corresponding thinking tools can be utilized to great advantage—especially when a quandary arises suddenly or appears novel. You will be well served by taking a few breaths, getting reliable consultation, and focusing on the salient issues. Psychologists Jeff Barnett and Brad Johnson (2008) recently offered a ten-stage ethical decision-making process model. Although a professional would be wise to progress through the stages sequentially, not all of the stages may be relevant to each situation, and it may be wise to return to earlier stages as new developments or vexing questions emerge. Barnett and Johnson's model includes the following:

- Define the situation clearly.
- Determine who will be impacted by the decision.
- Refer to your profession's code of ethics.
- Refer to relevant laws/regulations and professional guidelines.
- Reflect honestly on personal feelings and competence.
- Consult with trusted colleagues.
- Formulate alternative courses of action.
- Consider the possible outcomes for all parties involved.

- Consult with colleagues and ethics committees.
- Make a decision and monitor the outcome.

Whatever strategy or process you employ when responding to quandaries or formulating a decision with ethical implications, be sure to have a procedure to guide your efforts.

Key Components

- *Use an ethical decision-making process.*
- *Do not expect an ethics code to guide you to the "right" answer in any specific professional context.*
- *Remember that tools for thinking clearly and deliberately about ethical issues will be just as important as the ethics code.*
- *Refuse to rush to judgment or make snap decisions about the solutions to ethical quandaries.*

75
Consult Trustworthy Colleagues

Donnie was an insurance agent in a small Midwest community for more than 20 years. In all those years, nothing prepared him for the personal and professional crisis he encountered when a client, Charlie, was killed in an automobile accident. Until that fateful December evening when his car skidded out of control and collided with a tree, Charlie had been Donnie's good neighbor, fellow parishioner, and a life-insurance client for nearly 15 years. Donnie and his wife socialized with Charlie and his family. Nobody deserved Charlie's half-million-dollar insurance payout more than his wife. But now there was a problem. Donnie knew that Charlie's marriage was on the rocks, that Charlie had taken to drinking, and that he had become despondent and morose. Two weeks prior to the "accident," Charlie had his insurance coverage raised. Although there was no obvious smoking gun, Donnie suspected an insurance investigation would rule the accident a suicide. Donnie was torn between his obligations to his company, his professional code of ethics, and his deep loyalty to Charlie. After two sleepless nights, Donnie called a trusted colleague in the insurance business, someone

*for whom he had the utmost respect. He outlined the parameters of the
quandary. His colleague gave him excellent counsel, the kind you would
hope for from a dispassionate, experienced, and caring friend. It lowered
Donnie's anxiety, affirmed his own inclinations, and allowed him to proceed on a course that most aligned with his sense of professionalism.*

Here is the final element of ethics: Seek advice and assistance
from wise colleagues. Don't be misled by the placement of this element at the end of the book. Seeking consultation should be the
norm for professionals, not an exception. The evidence indicates that
professionals who get consultation make better ethical decisions than
those who go it alone. None of us can be expected to have the answer
to every problem or to have adequate expertise in the various specialties within our professions. Ethical decision making can be tough
under mundane circumstances. It can be daunting and distressing
when we have to deal with complex ethical conundrums, laced over
with our own powerful emotional reactions. Think of consultation as
an essential component of professional excellence. It suggests thorough regard for those we serve.

When the time comes to seek consultation, professionals can
draw on several guidelines for maximizing the value of this process.
First, use discretion in selecting a consultant. As we have previously
counseled, "When choosing a consultant, look for a seasoned colleague known for a strong commitment to the profession, sensitivity
to ethical matters, and a reputation for being both forthright and discreet" (Johnson & Ridley, 2004, p. 117). You want someone who can
give sound advice, make insightful connections, and facilitate the
process of ethical decision making. Whether the professional is a
member of your organization or a colleague with whom you have an
established relationship is secondary to the person's having the above
qualities. It is in your interest to establish a reciprocal consulting relationship with a highly trusted colleague. The relationship becomes
the context in which the two of you stand ready to assist each other
when quandaries arise.

Second, protect the anonymity of the person whose ethical behavior is problematic. The principles of confidentiality and privacy

hold even in cases involving ethically inappropriate behavior. The last thing you want to do is behave unethically in your attempt to resolve an ethical problem. Professionals who violate ethical standards and clients who become problematic nevertheless must be accorded the highest degree of ethical consideration in the process of ethical decision making. Here is a rule of thumb: If you are seeking consultation primarily because you want to share shocking or unusual material with someone, of if the temptation to share a juicy bit of gossip is powerful, you should probably reconsider. Ask yourself, "How will this consultation directly benefit the person with the problem?" "Has the person been informed that I will be seeking consultation?" "If not, have I changed enough of the detail in the case so that the individual could not possibly be identified?"

Finally, use the consultation for a professional tune-up. Find out if you inadvertently contribute to the onset of ethical problems. Determine if you have strayed beyond the boundaries of your own competence. Determine if there are preventative steps you might take. Get feedback on effective ways you can handle ethical problems once they surface. Of course, getting this kind of honest and penetrating consultation requires that you find a colleague who willingly tells you the truth.

Professionals who seek routine consultation make better decisions and offer more-effective services. They generally make better ethical decisions than those who attempt to solve difficult problems without assistance. The steps outlined above have proven utility. They are helpful in navigating the complex terrain of ethical problems.

Key Components

- *Seek advice and assistance from wise colleagues.*
- *Protect the anonymity of people embroiled in ethical problems.*
- *Fine-tune your ethical decision making through the assistance of consultants.*

References

American Psychological Association. (2002). Ethical principles of psychologists and code of conduct. *American Psychologist, 57,* 1060–1073.

Baier, K. (1958). *The moral point of view.* Ithaca, NY: Cornell University Press.

Bainton, R. H. (1995). *Here I stand: A life of Martin Luther.* New York: Plume.

Baker, E. K. (2003). *Caring for ourselves: A therapist's guide to personal and professional well-being.* Washington, D.C.: American Psychological Association.

Barnett, J., & Johnson, W. B. (2008). *Ethics desk reference for psychologists.* Washington, D.C.: American Psychological Association.

Bass, B. M., & Steidlmeier, P. (1999). Ethics, character, and authentic transformational leadership behavior. *Leadership Quarterly, 10,* 181–217.

Bayles, M. D. (1981). *Professional ethics.* Belmont, CA: Wadsworth.

Beauchamp, T. L., & Childress, J. F. (1994). *Principles of biomedical ethics (4th ed.).* Oxford, England: Oxford University Press.

Becker, T. E. (1998). Integrity in organizations: Beyond honesty and conscientiousness. *Academy of Management Review, 23,* 154–161.

Behnke, S. (2005). Reflecting on how we teach ethics. *APA Monitor, 36,* 64–65.

Behnke, S. (2006). Reflections on being an ethical clinician. *APA Monitor, 37,* 68–69.

Bellah, R. N., Madsen, R., Sullivan, W. M., & Swidler, A. (2007). *Habits of the heart: Individualism and commitment in American life.* Berkeley, CA: University of California Press.

Bennett, B. E., Bryant, B. K., VandenBos, G. R., & Greenwood, A. (1990). *Professional liability and risk management.* Washington, D.C.: American Psychological Association.

Berwick, D., et al. (2006). Technology for patient-centered, collaborative care. *Journal of Ambulatory Care Management, 29,* 1–2.

Beutler, L. E., & Bergan, J. (1991). Value change in counseling and psychotherapy: A search for scientific credibility. *Journal of Counseling Psychology, 38,* 16–24.

Bowden, P. (1997). *Caring: Gender-sensitive ethics.* London: Routledge & Kegan Paul.

Brock, P. (2008). *Charlatan: America's most dangerous huckster, the man who pursued him, and the age of flimflam.* New York: Crown.

Brown, R. D., & Krager, L. A. (1985). Ethical issues in graduate education. *Journal of Higher Education, 56,* 403–418.

Carver, G. W., & Kremer, G. R. (1991). *George Washington Carver: In his own words.* Columbia, MO: University of Missouri Press.

Ciulla, J. B. (1995). Leadership ethics: Mapping the territory. *Business Ethics Quarterly, 5,* 5–28.

Clark, C. R. (1993). Social responsibility ethics: Doing right, doing good, doing well. *Ethics and Behavior, 3,* 303–328.

Coombes, R. (2005). Senior doctors admit mistakes in campaign for more open culture. *BMJ, 331,* 595.

Corey G., Corey, M. S., & Callanan, P. (2006). *Issues and ethics in the helping professions (7th ed.).* Belmont, CA: Brooks-Cole.

Drane, J. F. (1994). Character and the moral life: A virtue approach to biomedical ethics. In E. R. DuBose, R. P. Hamel, & L. J. O'Connell (Eds.), *A matter of principles? Ferment in U. S. bioethics* (pp. 284–309). Valley Forge, PA: Trinity Press International.

Elkington, J. (1994). Towards the sustainable cooperation: Win-win-win business strategies for sustainable development. *California Management Review, 36,* 90–100.

Ellis, A. (1988). *How to stubbornly refuse to make yourself miserable about anything.* Secaucus, NJ: Lyle Stuart.

Epstein, R. M., & Hundert, E. M. (2002). Defining and assessing professional competence. *Journal of the American Medical Association, 287,* 226–235.

Farrow, A., Lang, J., & Frank, J. (2005). *Complicity: How the north promoted, prolonged, and profited from slavery.* New York: Ballantine Books.

Festinger, L. (1957). *A theory of cognitive dissonance.* Stanford, CA: Stanford University Press.

Gabbard, G. O. (1989). *Sexual exploitation in professional relationships.* Washington, D.C.: American Psychiatric Association.

Gladwell, M. (2002). *The tipping point: How little things can make a big difference.* New York: Back Bay Books.

Goleman, D. (1995). *Emotional intelligence.* New York: Bantam.

Heathfield, S. M. (2008). *Make no excuses.* http://humanresources.about.com/od/success/qt/no_excuses_s2.htm.

Holland, J. G. (1998). *Holland's life of Abraham Lincoln.* Lincoln, NE: University of Nebraska Press.

Johnson, W. B. (2003). A framework for conceptualizing competence to mentor. *Ethics and Behavior, 13,* 127–151.

Johnson, W. B., & Ridley, C. R. (2004). *The elements of mentoring.* New York: Palgrave Macmillan.

Kanungo, R., & Mendonca, M. (1996). *Ethical dimensions of leadership.* London: Sage.

Kaslow, N. J. (2004). Competencies in professional psychology. *American Psychologist, 59,* 774–781.

Katz, D., & Kahn, R. L. (1978). *The social psychology of organizations (2ⁿᵈ ed.)*. New York: Wiley.

Keith-Spiegel, P., Whitley, B. E., Balogh, D. W., Perkins, D. V., & Wittig, A. F. (2002). *The ethics of teaching: A casebook (2ⁿᵈ ed.)*. Mahwah, NJ: Lawrence Erlbaum.

King, M. L. (1964). Letter from Birmingham Jail. In *Why we can't wait*. New York: Harper & Row.

Kitchener, K. S. (1992). Psychologist as teacher and mentor: Affirming ethical values throughout the curriculum. *Professional Psychology: Research and Practice, 23,* 190–195.

Kitchener, K. S. (2000). *Foundations of ethical practice, research, and teaching in psychology*. Mahwah, NJ: Lawrence Erlbaum.

Koocher, G. P., & Keith-Spiegel, P. (1998). *Ethics in psychology: Professional standards and cases (2nd ed)*. New York: Oxford University Press.

Lawrence, D. H. (1915/1989). *The rainbow*. Cambridge University Press: Cambridge, England.

Lindbergh, A. M. (1955). *Gift from the sea: An answer to the conflict in our lives*. New York: Pantheon.

Lovett, F. (1997). Thinking about values (report of December 13, 1996, *Wall Street Journal* national survey). *The Responsive Community, 7,* 87.

Lowe, J. (1999). *Michael Jordon speaks: Lessons from the world's greatest champion*. New York: Wiley.

Maslow, A. H. (1943). A theory of human motivation. *Psychological Review, 50,* 370–396.

Meara, N. M., Schmidt, L. D., & Day, J. D. (1996). Principles and virtues: A foundation for ethical decisions, policies, and character. *The Counseling Psychologist, 24,* 4–77.

Milgram, S. (1974). *Obedience to authority*. New York: Harper and Row.

Myer, D. G. (2007). *Exploring Social Psychology (4ᵗʰ ed.)*. New York: McGraw-Hill.

Noddings, N. (1984). *Caring: A feminine approach to ethics and moral education*. Berkeley, CA: University of California Press.

Patterson, C. H. (1985). *The therapeutic relationship*. Monterey, CA: Brooks/Cole.

Pojman, L. P. (1999). *Ethics: Discovering right and wrong*. Belmont, CA: Wadsworth.

Pope, K. S., & Vetter, V. A. (1992). Ethical dilemmas encountered by members of the American Psychological Association: A national survey. *American Psychologist, 47,* 397–411.

Porter, M. (2002). http://tartarus.org/~martin/essays/burkequote.html.

Prilleltensky, I. (2000). Value-based leadership in organizations: Balancing values, interests, and power among citizens. *Ethics & Behavior, 10,* 139–158.

Ridley, C. R. (2005). *Overcoming unintentional racism in counseling and therapy: A practitioner's guide to intentional intervention (2nd ed.)*. Thousand Oaks, CA: Sage.

Ridley, C. R., Ethington, L. W., & Heppner, P. P. (2007). Cultural confrontation: A skill of advanced cultural empathy. In P. B. Pedersen, J. Draguns, W. Loner, & J. Trimble (Eds.), *Counseling across cultures (3rd ed.,* pp. 377–393). Thousand Oaks, CA: Sage.

Ridley, C. R., Liddle, M. C., Hill, C. L., & Li, L. C. (2000). Ethical decision making in multicultural counseling. In J. Ponterotto, J. M. Casas, L. A. Suzuki, & C. M. Alexander (Eds.), *Handbook of multicultural counseling (2nd ed.,* pp. 165–185). Thousand Oaks, CA: Sage.

Rogers, C. R. (1961). *On becoming a person.* Boston: Houghton Mifflin.

Rogers, C. R. (1962). The interpersonal relationship: The core of guidance. *Harvard Educational Review, 32,* 416–429.

Russell, H. (1964). Ethical obligations in the student-professor relationship. *The Journal of Risk and Insurance, 31,* 393–403.

Rutter, P. (1989). *Sex in the forbidden zone.* New York: Fawcett Crest.

Searle, J. R. (1995). *The construction of social reality.* New York: Free Press.

Shoda, Y., Mischel, W., & Peake, P. K. (1990). Predicting adolescent cognitive and self-regulatory competencies from preschool delay of gratification: Identifying diagnostic conditions. *Developmental Psychology, 26,* 978–986.

Smedes, L. B. (1983). *Mere morality: What god expects from ordinary people.* Grand Rapids, MI: Eerdmans.

Smith, D. (2003). 10 ways practitioners can avoid ethical pitfalls. *APA Monitor on Psychology, 34 (1),* 50–51.

Sperry, L. (2007). *The ethical and professional practice of counseling and psychotherapy.* Boston: Pearson/Allyn and Bacon.

Strunk, W., & White, E. B. (2000). *The elements of style (4th ed.).* Boston: Allyn & Bacon.

Sue, D. W., & Sue, D. (2002). *Counseling the culturally diverse: Theory and practice.* New York: Wiley.

Tabachnick, B. G., Keith-Spiegel, P., & Pope, K. S. (1991). Ethics of teaching. *American Psychologist, 46,* 506–515.

United States Government. (1979). *The Belmont Report: Ethical principles and guidelines for the protection of human subjects of research.* Washington, DC.

Watzlawick, P., Beavin, J. H., & Jackson, D. D. (1967). *Pragmatics of human communication: A study of interactional patterns, pathologies, and paradoxes.* New York: W. W. Norton & Company.

Welfel, E. R., & Patterson, L. E. (2005). *The counseling process: A multitheoretical integrative approach (6th ed.).* Belmont, CA: Thomson.

White, L. P., & Wooten, K. C. (1986). *Professional ethics and practice in organizational development: A systematic analysis of issues, alternatives, and approaches.* New York: Praeger.

Wood, R., & Power, C. (1987). Aspects of the competence-performance distinction: Educational, psychological, and measurement issues. *Journal of Curricular Studies, 19,* 409–424.

Zimbardo, P. G. (1969). The human choice: Individuation, reason, and order versus deindividuation, impulse, and chaos. *Nebraska Symposium on Motivation, 17,* 237–307.

Index